University Intellectual Property

A Source of Finance and Impact

Edited by Graham Richards

HARRIMAN HOUSE LTD

3A Penns Road
Petersfield
Hampshire
GU32 2EW
GREAT BRITAIN

Tel: +44 (0)1730 233870
Fax: +44 (0)1730 233880
Email: enquiries@harriman-house.com
Website: www.harriman-house.com

First published in Great Britain in 2012

Copyright © Harriman House 2012

The right of Graham Richards to be identified as the Author has been asserted in accordance with the Copyright, Design and Patents Act 1988.

ISBN: 9780857192325

British Library Cataloguing in Publication Data
A CIP catalogue record for this book can be obtained from the British Library.

Figure data and information copyright © respective owners and sources
Final figure design and presentation copyright © Harriman House Ltd

Set in Minion, League Gothic and HelveticaNeue.

Printed and bound by CPI Group (UK) Ltd, Croydon, CR0 4YY.

Contents

About the Contributors

Graham Richards was head of Chemistry at the University of Oxford. He was the scientific founder of Oxford Molecular Group Plc and is senior non-executive director of IP Group Plc.

Professor Sir Robin Jacob is Hugh Loddie Professor of Intellectual Property Law at University College London. After practising at the Intellectual Property Bar he became a Patent Judge and was appointed a Lord Justice of Appeal.

Ian Bingham is a Rolls-Royce trained Aeronautical Engineer and Patent Attorney who specialises in the creation and exploitation of commercially-focused Intellectual property.

Patricia Barclay is a lawyer specialising in the commercialisation of scientific invention. Before opening her own firm, Bonaccord, she worked as General Counsel of two multinationals and a start-up.

Roya Ghafele worked as an economist with the United Nation's World Intellectual Property Organisation (WIPO) and is now the director of Oxfirst Ltd.

Alexander Weedon joined UCL BioMedica, the predecessor to UCL Business, in 2004 and now manages a team responsible for providing IP and legal support to the Business Managers and UCL. He obtained a first degree in Biochemistry and has Masters degrees in Intellectual Property Management and International Business Law.

Catherine Rhodes is a Research Fellow in Science Ethics at the Institute for Science, Ethics and Innovation, School of Law, University of Manchester. She has a background in international relations and her main area of research is the international governance of biotechnology.

Preface

Universities are being forced to look beyond their traditional roles of teaching and conducting original research. The driving force behind this is above all financial pressure, as governments, fee payers and other investors seek to limit their contributions or produce a more tangible result for the money they have given. In the search for extra finance and impact, the attention of universities is increasingly focused on the exploitation of intellectual property generated by the academics working within them, but the situation is complex. The sorts of questions that have to be answered are: What constitutes intellectual property? Who owns it? How can it best be exploited?

This book aims to answer these questions by drawing upon the experiences of practitioners in this area. This will be helpful to academics, university administrators, and those involved in the growing business that is technology transfer. This latter activity involves not just those within universities, but also business angels, venture capitalists and major companies which increasingly look towards academic research to bolster their knowledge. All of these groups will find useful ideas, that will clarify thinking on university IP, in this book.

After a review of the recent history and the current situation, this book presents the views and experiences of a series of experts in this field. These range from those of a very senior lawyer, a patent attorney and a solicitor, to the views of a set of practitioners involved in technology transfer. In the last chapter, a provocative look at the ethics of the situation is presented.

We hope that the pieces in this collection will help readers to navigate this increasingly important area, which is now seen as a measure of the impact a university has as well as a potential source of finance for the institution.

Graham Richards,

June 2012

1. Introduction

By Graham Richards

I am not a lawyer, but nonetheless I have had considerable experience of the exploitation of university intellectual property (IP) in some 50 years at Oxford University – where I chaired the very large Chemistry Department – and extended periods in California at Stanford University and at University of California, Berkeley. I was directly responsible for the creation of several spin-out companies from university research departments, have acted as a non-executive director or chairman of several more, and have been associated with perhaps another 50 companies created on the basis of university IP.

The current economic situation, where governments are unlikely to be able to fund universities to a level at which they would wish, makes it increasingly certain that universities will look to their intellectual property as a source of finance. The most important reasons for the existence of universities are to provide teaching and to perform original research, but this third leg of IP exploitation is certainly going to grow in importance.

This increasing pursuit of commercialisation of research need not undermine the other work that universities do. Professor G. H. Hardy of Trinity College, Cambridge may have toasted the Cambridge Mathematical Society as follows: 'Here's to pure mathematics. May it never be applied', but his wish was in vain because there is no branch of science of which one can be sure that it will never have any practical application. As another wise man once said, 'there are only two sorts of research: applied research and yet to be applied research'.

Indeed, the most successful and financially rewarding returns from the exploitation of intellectual property have in fact arisen from blue-sky research, so there is no reason for a change in emphasis towards exploitation [of intellectual property] to cause academics to modify their choices of research topic. They just need to be aware, as does their department and the central university, of the possibilities, pitfalls and mechanisms in the area of exploiting university IP. My experience has shown that as universities and their academics look to exploit the IP they have developed, they are going to come up against a number of problems. This is because the situation regarding the ownership of IP generated in universities is unclear in many instances and the system of rewards for academics and their students if the exploitation is successful is even less straightforward.

> **There is no reason for a change in emphasis towards exploitation [of intellectual property] to cause academics to modify their choices of research topic.**

Part of this confusion is over patents and a lot of energy is usually expended in resolving disputes that arise in this area. However, there are other key areas too and if we are going to have sensible policies, preferably standardised across the sector, that lead to benefits for both institutions and individuals then copyright, trade marks, and even consulting and advising, should be included in government and university policy.

In this book I intend, with the help of experienced colleagues, to try to clarify the situation with regard to intellectual property and reward structures for those who create it. We also suggest what might be sensible modifications to the current practices so as to increase the value of returns and to achieve the fairness which most academics can endorse.

2. The Confused Situation

By Graham Richards

To begin this chapter, it may be helpful to give a brief account of my own involvement in this area over the 50 years I spent as an academic in Oxford. After this account I will describe the different forms of intellectual property that academics and universities are involved with and look at why the situation as it stands is confused; as will be seen, the status quo involves a plethora of varied policies and approaches. The views of others on these issues then follow in subsequent chapters.

Personal story

The British government of Harold Wilson, buoyed up by Wilson's slogan of the *white hot technological revolution*, which he coined in an attempt to revitalise the UK economy, decreed that universities should create University and Industry Committees to foster the then not very active boundary between the two sectors.

In 1978 I became chairman of the committee, succeeding my entrepreneurial mathematical colleague Alan Tayler. There was very little happening in terms of interaction between universities and the commercial world at the time. Oxford's rules prohibited academics from consulting on university-headed notepaper and as far as patents were concerned, the university stated that it neither owned nor sought to own intellectual property derived from work done in the university by its employees.

This attitude derived from the fact that Oxford was totally dominated by the avoidance of any risk to itself. This obsession in turn arose as the result of an infamously damaging case in the 1920s when an academic got the institution into an expensive mess as a result of fraudulent activity. This incident – the *Owen case* – is described in detail in a later chapter, but suffice it to say for now that so serious were the ramifications that Oxford and its sister university, Cambridge, were seeking to avoid any involvement with intellectual property.

So it was that one of my first acts as chairman of the University and Industry Committee was to take out insurance, very cheaply obtained, to cover the university against claims arising from academics doing consultancy. The old system probably would not have protected Oxford anyway.

The first modern spin-out and IP Group

When in the late 1980s the university did begin to claim ownership of intellectual property following a law change during Mrs Thatcher's premiership, I started the first of the modern spin-out companies where the university had as of right some of the equity as a result of its contribution of IP. This was Oxford Molecular Ltd, founded in 1989. That company had an initial public offering (IPO) in 1994 before being sold in two parts in 2000. It is worth noting that the University benefitted to the tune of £10 million from that company.

When I became head of the Chemistry Department at Oxford in 1997, the big item in my in-tray was the building of a new research laboratory. This required raising some £64 million and this was achieved with a novel source of funding; the City of London company Beeson Gregory provided some £20 million up front in return for half of the university's equity in spin-out companies created in the Chemistry Department for a period of 15 years, with a similar arrangement for licences. In the decade following the deal, set up in the year 2000, some 15 companies were formed of which five have gone public after successful IPOs. Both Beeson Gregory and Oxford have benefitted significantly from the arrangement.

Beeson Gregory, following a merger with Evolution, then went on to create a subsidiary to replay aspects of the deal with other universities. This separate company, initially named IP2IPO Ltd, later IP Group Plc, has partnerships with a dozen UK universities and has been responsible for the founding of some 70 companies, of which a dozen are now publicly owned following IPOs.

I was chairman of IP2IPO Plc for a time and am now senior non-executive director of IP Group, and in addition I am or have been a non-executive director of six university spin-out companies. I was also in large part responsible for the founding of Oxford University's technology transfer office, Isis Innovation, and a director thereof for 20 years. This has given me a wide overview of the field of university IP development and commercialisation. In my work, I have seen that of the several forms of intellectual property it is the case of patents which has been most closely followed and so it is to these that I will now turn.

Patents

The Patents Act of 1977 in the UK placed the ownership of intellectual property generated by employees who were expected to produce patented work to their employer. In the case of industrial companies this is fairly straightforward: if you work for a pharmaceutical company in a research department, then developing new drugs is your job and your employer obviously expects to receive the rewards. Universities are less clear cut and accordingly the switch from individual academics owning the intellectual property arising from research in their laboratories to that ownership being vested in the employing university was not without contention. Is, for instance, an academic researcher *expected* to produce IP?

It may be hard to convince academics that the IP on work which they have done in their own research laboratory should belong to the university and that this is preferable for all concerned, but the latter part of this is in fact true, although perhaps not obvious at first sight. For example, if the individual is the owner, then he or she will have to pay all the patent and legal costs, whereas if the institution owns the IP then it will have to pay the expenses. Initial expenses are not large but once the international phase is reached these can become significant. A real danger of individual ownership is that patents are allowed to lapse, which is the worst of all possible scenarios as it means no ownership and alerting the rest of the world to the invention.

> **❝ It may be hard to convince academics that the IP on work which they have done in their own research laboratory should belong to the university and that this is preferable for all concerned. ❞**

Most universities across the world now own the patent IP of their employees. What is much less universal is the situation with respect to the work done by students. If the uncertainty is not avoided then there are real problems when exploiting the research: a student could at some late stage turn up and claim to have done the work and give evidence in terms of joint authorship of publications. The prospect of this can be a severe impediment to financial backers.

Although it is best if the central institution owns all aspects of the IP and has mechanisms for technology transfer, it is equally important that all who contribute to developing the IP should have incentives and rewards. If exploitation is in the form of creating a spin-out company, then the responsible researchers should receive equity, the percentages being settled by negotiation, with the academics being reasonable and ideally having their own legal adviser.

If on the other hand the mechanism of exploitation is by licensing the IP to other companies then there needs to be a scale of remuneration dependent on the income. The Oxford system which I helped devise gives virtually all the early income to the researcher as an incentive to seeking patent protection, but then a sliding scale so that as the sums become larger the percentage going to the university increases. In the rare case where the invention brings in millions of pounds, then both the individuals and the institution will receive comparable amounts.

Copyright

If the situation with respect to patents is less than totally satisfactory, then the copyright situation is even more in need of clarification and change, although when this occurs it is certain to generate opposition, especially if the university has a share in or ownership of the copyright.

When a scientist working in a university laboratory discovers something which leads to a patent, it is now generally accepted that both the researcher and the employing university should share the rewards on an equitable basis. If, on the other hand, one of the colleagues of the inventive scientist spends all his or her time writing text books on the subject for which they are paid to teach and do research, then universally the royalties go wholly to the author. This does not seem fair because the sums of money can be quite considerable; there are academic authors who earn hundreds of thousands of pounds per year from writing standard texts. This is very much what academics should do, but it seems far from clear why synthesising a molecule of commercial value should lead to income sharing while writing books or articles should not. Why should universities own patent rights but not copyright?

Of course it is somewhat complicated by the fact that academics do not have set hours of work. The boundary between what is really part of one's duties as a lecturer or professor and what is totally outside employment in a specific department is very fuzzy. However, if one takes the case of an academic historian, hired to cover a set period of history, who then writes books on this topic and makes magnificently remunerated television programmes, then it is hard to see why the employer should not derive some benefit.

A further level of complexity is now developing as a result of the internet and the use of IT by lecturers. Increasingly the contemporary student does not like lectures using traditional talk and chalk. Blackboards are even considered to provide a health and safety hazard. White boards and the provision of lecture notes on the web in the form of handouts are now expected. But who owns these lecture notes, the lecturer or the employing university? Some of these notes will be downloaded from the internet by lecturers at universities in other countries, either directly or via students who move on to teaching posts. Once more it is hard to see why there is any essential difference between this type of work and scientific research, given that the formal duties of the academic are to teach and to do research. If the university were to own the teaching materials then they can employ a mechanism whereby the content is protected and exploited to the mutual benefit of both author and employer.

Trade marks

Universities have often been very lax in protecting their names and symbols such as their crests. Oxford is a case in point as it failed to register the coat of arms of the university which had been in use for centuries and so had to develop a variant with a belt drawn around it, which was subsequently protected. The crest without the belt appears on tee-shirts and other items sold across the world, with no royalty on the proceeds due to the university.

An even more surprising omission was the fact that Oxford's enormously successful publishing house, Oxford University Press, which dates from 1473, did not protect its name until the 1960s. At that time Robert Maxwell decided to publish an *Oxford Dictionary of Spelling*. The university took his company to court on the grounds that the book was passing itself off as being from the University Press. They lost. It was decided to appeal and fortunately for the university the case came up before the sparkling eyes of Lord Denning.

The corporate entity bringing the case was 'The Chancellor, Masters and Scholars of the University of Oxford'. Denning observed that he was a plaintiff being both a Master, having the degree of MA, and a former scholar of the university, but neither side objected. The case of Maxwell's company was that it was indeed based in Oxford so that the title of the work was accurate. Lord Denning observed that the defendants were located in the suburb of Headington and that the university would not object if the defendants' work were called the *Headington Dictionary of Spelling*. The defendants lost in the appeal.

Another similar tale involves a pharmaceutical company based in Boston tried to use the name 'Veritas', the Harvard motto, but were prevented by the university, becoming instead Vertex. Nonetheless some bright young man in the UK did in fact register the name for use in Europe.

These anecdotes, though slightly comic, do illustrate just how careful academic bodies need to be to defend their trade marks and names. Perhaps the area where most care needs to be taken in registering names is with domain names for use on the internet. Many institutions have suffered at the hands of unscrupulous souls who register obvious names in advance of the legitimate body getting around to the task.

Consultancy

Consulting and giving expert advice, such as when acting as an expert witness, are further somewhat muddy realms where income, often very significant, can be earned by academics by virtue of their employment by their host institution. Although many academics would complain were the university employer to take a proportion of such income, it is hard to see why the employer should not have some rights.

In addition, if a professionally-run organisation manages and organises the consultancies on behalf of academics, it is quite likely that even after this body has taken a percentage the professors can be much better rewarded. This is because academics are notoriously bad at negotiating fees for consultancies and similar activities. I like to recount the tale, probably not apocryphal, of the Oxford academic who was invited to appear on a BBC television programme for a fee of £50. He wrote back immediately accepting the invitation and enclosing his cheque.

Academic lawyers can, not infrequently, receive large sums in arbitration cases, but they would not have been selected were it not for the post they hold in a Law Faculty.

In such areas there is a strong case to be made for these outside activities being properly organised by the university, which would then take some financial benefit. Instituting change along these lines, however, would certainly generate opposition.

Summary

As we have seen, it is really only in the field of patents and licensing that university intellectual property has begun to generate significant income. Even this activity has a relatively short history, with a marked difference between what has happened in the USA and in Britain. This is the subject to which the next chapter turns.

3. Bayh-Dole-Thatcher

By Graham Richards

The Bayh-Dole Act

In 1980 the United States became concerned about declining productivity and rising competition from Japan. As a response Congress passed the Bayh-Dole Act, which enabled universities to patent federally-funded research and pursue ownership of an invention in preference to the government. Universities were thus offered the opportunity to licence campus-based inventions to private companies in exchange for royalties. In the years following, Congress passed a number of additional laws to encourage university-industry links, notably generous tax breaks for corporations willing to invest in academic research.

There are those who were unhappy about the Bayh-Dole Act since in a sense giving private firms the rights to inventions generated at public expense means that the public has to pay twice for the same invention – once through taxes to support the research that yielded the invention and then again through higher monopoly prices and restricted supply when the invention reaches the market. However, the legislation does contain safeguards, such as a *march-in* provision enabling the federal government to terminate an exclusive licence if the licensee fails to take effective steps to bring the invention into practical application within three years. A royalty-free licence is also included to enable the government to use the technology at any time.

What is quite certain is that the Act produced a massive increase in the amount of academic research being commercialised in the USA, more in terms of licensing than in the creation of spin-out companies. There was a ten-fold increase in patents generated and cumulative increases in industry funding for universities, rising to an annual $2 billion by the turn of the millennium. In June 2011, however, the US Supreme Court in Stanford *v* Roche cut back the effect of Bayh-Dole. Quite how much remains to be seen.

The Thatcher initiative

The much-repeated truism that Britain is good at invention, but poor at exploitation, is based on a long history of innovative science and woeful commercial success. In the 19th century Perkin produced the first synthetic dye, mauveine, and even started to manufacture it commercially. The country had a unique lead but by 1914 when it was necessary to send an army to France, the only source of khaki dye for the uniforms was I.G. Farbenindustrie and some of the British Expeditionary force went to war in navy blue uniforms dyed with woad, the natural dye favoured by the ancient Britons.

The BBC started television broadcasts in 1938, some ten years before a television service began in the USA, but by the end of the 1960s there were no British companies making TV sets. Computing is often traced back to Babbage, but the first modern computer was built at Bletchley as part of the Enigma code cracking project by Tommy Flowers, based on the theoretical work of Alan Turing. In the early 1960s possibly the best electronic computers in the world were built by the UK Ferranti company. My own first experience of computing was with the wonderful Ferranti Mercury in 1962. By the 1970s the industry had disappeared overseas.

The modern era was much influenced by the second world war. In the dark days of 1941 when Britain stood alone after the fall of France, the USA came to the aid of the old country by providing 50 ships to help make up for convoy losses in the Atlantic. The deal was known as lend-lease, since at its heart was the provision of permanent leases on bases in the West Indies to the Americans. Less widely known is the fact that in the small print of the agreement between Churchill and Roosevelt, the UK agreed not to patent three strategic British inventions: radar, the jet engine and penicillin. All were potentially vital to the war effort and only the USA had the industrial power to exploit these technologies. They helped the allies to win the war, but at huge financial loss to post-war Britain.

That fact was not lost on the post-war Atlee British government which in 1948 set up the National Research for Development Corporation (the NRDC). This Quango was created to commercialise innovations resulting from publicly-funded research at government research centres and universities, with research support from the state-funded research councils. Amongst their successes were the pyrethroid insecticides developed at Rothamsted; the cephalosporin antibiotics, from the same Oxford laboratories which had exploited penicillin; magnetic resonance imaging; and Interferon. The NRDC became the British Technology Group (BTG) following a merger with the National Enterprise Board and was privatised in 1992.

In its days as a state monopoly the NRDC, despite a few big successes, was essentially risk averse, bureaucratic and not subject to normal commercial pressures. Most notoriously it failed to patent monoclonal antibodies, although it is not clear exactly who was to blame for that mistake which perhaps cost the UK Treasury hundreds of millions of pounds.

❝ In 1987 Margaret Thatcher took a seminal decision to hand over the ownership of intellectual property derived from government funding to the universities in which the IP had been generated. ❞

This happened under the premiership of Margaret Thatcher who had great sensitivity to commercialisation (she was an Oxford-trained chemist as well as a lawyer).

Indeed, virtually nothing happened in the UK regarding university IP exploitation until Mrs Thatcher shook up the system. She had been responsible for a crucial innovation in the tax rules to encourage venture capital. In 1987 she [Margaret Thatcher] took a seminal decision to hand over the ownership of intellectual property derived from government funding to the universities in which the IP had been generated, provided they set up a mechanism to encourage exploitation, or has it has become known *technology transfer*. This was a British version of Bayh-Dole because universities were funded by the government. This crucial step set the stage for the flowering of spin-out companies in the UK.

A current perspective

It is now 30 years since the Bayh-Dole Act and 25 since Mrs Thatcher's equivalent revolutionary change in the UK. Many feel that the time is ripe to revisit the scene. A number of credible and influential individuals and august professional bodies have expressed concerns as to whether other forms of knowledge transfer might be impeded by the system we have in place and that commercialisation might damage the prime mission of universities to pursue fundamental knowledge, even if only by steering research away from curiosity-driven projects.

The National Academy of Sciences view

The influential US body, the National Academy of Sciences (NAS) in 2010 undertook a major investigation into the management of university IP in the public interest. The principal findings support the Bayh-Dole process, above all because it removed inconsistencies and gave rise to the surge in patenting and licensing activity. Further, the findings suggested that academic norms do not seem to have been undermined. In a very long and thorough report the committee did nonetheless make a series of recommendations aimed at reducing tensions which might occur between the various university goals of knowledge dissemination, regional economic development, service to faculty, generation of revenue for the institution and addressing humanitarian needs.

One of the suggested moves was the creation of a clear mission statement and the setting up of standing advisory committees, with the technology transfer office being accountable to the university's research management with a formal code of good practice. The committee was also strongly of the view that the exchange of scientific materials should be made simpler. Standardised terms for licensing university technology to start-up enterprises were suggested as well. Overall, though, the report is supportive of the Bayh-Dole Act.

The Manchester Manifesto

In the UK a group originating in the University of Manchester's Institute for Science Ethics and Innovation produced a much more radical document, posing the question 'Who owns Science?'

In a later chapter of this book the group explain their views more fully, but it is worth noting that most of the signatories to the manifesto are philosophers and ethicists rather than scientists. One major exception to this is the prominent name of Nobel laureate Sir John Sulston, who led the research into the sequencing of the human genome at Hinxton near Cambridge. No doubt his views must have been coloured by the extraordinary antics of some commercial bodies in trying to patent genes, even when they had no idea of their function or possible use. Nonetheless the views of such an eminent scientist carry considerable weight.

Certainly the question of what can be patented needs constant monitoring, but it may be worth remembering that Sulston's own work was funded in large part by The Wellcome Trust whose wealth ultimately derives from the pharmaceutical patents taken out by The Wellcome Foundation.

The importance of balance

Particularly in the area of patents and above all in the field of health, drugs, diagnostics and devices, there are inevitable tensions among parties with competing interests. Scientists want their work to be published as soon as possible and to receive recognition; companies who have invested in research do not want rivals to benefit from their investment without contributing; the public wants drugs to be as cheap as possible and people of a generous spirit would like the poor countries of the world to benefit from research on purely humanitarian grounds; and investors in new companies will not provide funds unless they have some certainty that the newly created entity is protected from copying by rivals. Finding the correct balance between all these interests is far from easy.

Scientists are naïf if they take a simplistic view. Often they see themselves as particularly exploited, but even that is not universally true and it is worth remembering that there are academic rogues who are just as malevolent as the most avaricious companies.

4. Academic Rogues

By Graham Richards

The outside world, and perhaps particularly industry, often views academics as rather unworldly, naïf and fundamentally gentle souls. Nothing could be further from the truth. The university sector, and in particular science, is a competitive game and one which is much less closely regulated than most economic sectors.

All experienced academics know of colleagues who have elbowed and even cheated their way to preferment and who have done down colleagues. In my own early experience I recall putting in a grant application which was turned down by an eminent referee in the days when one could recognise a particular typewriter's output. My proposed experiment was supposedly deemed *impossible*, but within months the referee had published the same piece of work as his own.

In my area of research there was a trick played successfully on one of my colleagues who had a track record of devising novel, exciting experiments. On publishing one such breakthrough, he received a flattering letter from a researcher in the same field with a high reputation. The letter said how impressed the writer was with the work, particularly as he himself had done the same experiment and had been just about to publish himself but had been pipped at the post. He went on to say that the next obvious step could be something that the original author was bound to be about to do and proposing that they should collaborate rather than compete. My colleague agreed and did virtually all the work, but when it came time to publish this extension in a major paper the writer of the flattering letter became very awkward and insisted on being the first author, as it had been *his* idea. My colleague learned that this scientist had played the same trick on a number of other innovators.

Some scientists can play very rough. One of the most distinguished British chemists was known in his early days to go to the apparatus of a laboratory colleague and rip out a pump during the night so as to be able to use it immediately notwithstanding wrecking a colleague's experiment. The same man once visited a major laboratory, saw what was being done with a novel piece of equipment and then returned to his own lab, bribed the technicians to work overtime and then hurried to rush out a publication on the subject so as to establish priority.

When it comes to the commercialisation of research, the lax governance under which academics operate has enabled quite a number to take intellectual property which rightly belonged to their universities, but to ignore this and just to set up companies as if they owned the IP. Occasionally they have even been known to do this in a foreign country.

The Owen Case

The most flagrant case of academic misbehaviour is probably the Owen scandal at Oxford University, which was so grotesque that it had a major and long-lasting impact on the commercialisation of research.

Following the first world war the British government was sensibly concerned about food production. In 1924 the Ministry of Agriculture established and funded an Institute of Agricultural Engineering at Oxford University, whilst pressuring the administration to appoint one of the Ministry's own employees as the director: Professor Brynor James Owen. It was not long before it became clear that where money was concerned Owen was, at the very least, devious. By the end of his first year the university's auditors were informing the Vice-Chancellor that they found the finances of the institute difficult to fathom.

For the following four years Owen continued to make the finances opaque with significant blurring of the distinction between his own private income and that of his institute. In the university committee hierarchy, Owen's institute was overseen by the Committee for Rural Economy, which was increasingly concerned by the size of the overdraft of the institute. In 1929 the committee realised that £22,000 was missing from their institute's accounts, but was present in those of a company Sugar Beet & Crop Driers, which had earlier bought patents from Owen (whose research concerned the extraction of sugar from sugar beet). Owen managed to convince his supervising committee that this money would be placed in a trust which he was forming on behalf of his institute and which would receive the money due to him for the patents. The committee even allowed Owen to be a technical advisor to Sugar Beet & Crop Driers with a salary, large for the period, of £3000 per year plus 2.5% of profits, never to be less than £1000 for five years.

Owen meanwhile was describing the institute accounts, kept at Coutts in London, as his own while being secretly kept in the university's name. By 1930 these were overdrawn by £16,000. The university did nothing even though from Owen's own reports it knew that he had erected a sugar beet factory in the village of Eynsham some six miles outside Oxford.

It was not until 1931 that the Registrar of the University, Sir Douglas Veale, heard from a friend in the Ministry of Agriculture that Owen had forged letters from the Ministry and from the Treasury. Owen was suspended but this was not the end of the affair. In 1931 Sugar Beet & Crop Driers, with two other plaintiffs, sued the university for the colossal sum of £750,000 on the grounds that the patents sold by Owen to the company were fraudulent in claiming the superiority of methods of extracting sugar, which was not true. Since the university's name gave creditability to the patents and Owen was its agent, it was seen as liable. The patents were in fact worthless, which led to heavy losses for the company. The company suffered further losses by following the advice of Owen, who was acting with consent of the university and on its behalf.

A huge potential loss

The threat of a £750,000 loss hung over the university until 1939 when the case was settled out of court for £75,000. This was a sum many times larger than the government grant to the university but Veale was successful at a special tribunal in persuading the government that it should shoulder most of the blame, leaving the university to find the smaller, but still significant for the time, sum of £25,000.

This scandal was however not the limit of Owen's wrong doing. Following a conference of British Empire Prime Ministers he went to the office of International Harvester Company of Great Britain (IHC Ltd) and said that his Oxford institute had been commissioned by the Imperial Conference to nominate firms from whom 100,000 tractors costing £65,000 ($325,000 at the then current conversion rate) would be purchased to carry out a four-year plan of Empire Development. In their eagerness to be accepted IHC Ltd agreed to give Owen £30,000 to conduct experiments. All this was backed up by documents on stationery headed 'Treasury' and 'Imperial Conferences' and he even gave himself a doctorate. He persuaded the Ministry of Agriculture to pay for a visit to the USA to study advanced methods in agricultural schools. When he returned to England he made up the story that his wife had inherited an annual income of £50,000 from a long-lost mother who had oil wealth. This accounted for his lifestyle when his university salary was only £1000 per year.

The International Harvester Company of America became concerned and its assistant treasurer confronted Owen who remarked "Does this mean that the company doubts my bona fides?" Somewhat contemptuously Owen offered to repay all the money IHC Ltd had advanced and wrote out a cheque for $150,000 asking if the company wanted this with all that such a transaction would imply. They did, but the cheque bounced.

The court case

Owen then became involved with the Ford Motor Company who were keen to have the order for the Imperial Conference tractors, although they were surprised that such a large order should be placed in one go. Owen talked his way out of this and persuaded Ford to advance $170,000 for his institute's experiments, giving him enough to cover the cheque to IHC and $20,000 for himself. At precisely this time Oxford finally suspended Owen and on hearing this Ford contacted Owen, who was at the time staying in a luxury hotel in Cannes. He told Ford that his Oxford suspension was due to a personal quarrel which would not affect Ford's nomination. It then became clear that the letterheads and supporting documents were fraudulent and Owen was arrested and appeared at Bow Street Police Court. He pleaded not guilty and said to the Chief Magistrate, Sir Charles Biron, "I have a perfect answer to these outrageous charges".

At his trial at the Old Bailey he was found guilty and sentenced to four years penal servitude. Legend had it that while he was in prison, Owen swindled some of the wardens of their savings. Prison was the end of Owen's career, but the ramifications for Oxford University and the wider academic entrepreneurial world were more long-lasting.

As a result of the near catastrophic impact of the Owen affair Oxford and Cambridge, at the time the overwhelmingly dominant institutions in Britain, were terrified of a repeat incident. Thus even when I was first an Oxford academic in the mid-1960s, the university policy was that it neither owned nor sought to own the intellectual property of work done by me or my colleagues even though it might have been performed in university laboratories, using university equipment and technicians. The whole system was dominated by the fear of risk.

The UK Patent Act

The 1977 Patents Act made it quite clear that employers own the intellectual property of work done by their employees. For most universities, as with companies, this clarified the situation and almost universally institutions make claim for inventions made by their employees. Immediately after the passing of the Act, Oxford and Cambridge universities attempted to retain the old system by handing the IP back to individual researchers.

> " The 1977 Patents Act made it quite clear that employers own the intellectual property of work done by their employees. "

This is not as generous as it seems since the costs of patenting them falls on the researcher rather than his or her employer. Although a small number of significant companies have emerged from the laissez faire approach, in general it is unwise. Patent costs are initially not very significant, but once one reaches the national phase after a couple of years, then the costs become onerous. If the patent holder drops the patent at that stage then we have the worst of all possible worlds: as has been mentioned earlier the work is then unprotected, but the wider community has been alerted to its existence and possible value.

Changing the culture was not achieved over night. In Oxford the system was modified in stages over a period of a dozen years so that now all work done by its employees and its students belongs to the university, albeit with the duty to exploit or, if not, let the employee have the IP.

Cambridge took rather longer to reach similar conclusions and still does not lay claim to work by students. Although such an attitude may seem to be one of generosity, in practice it is a real hindrance to exploitation since there may be a residual fear that having funded a venture, it may be possible for a student to turn up claiming part ownership of patents. This fear can discourage inventors.

In general, however, universities at last do have coherent policies on intellectual property and in-house professionals to negotiate royalties or equity shares in spin-out companies. The business world has at last realised that academics are not selfless saints, but prone to all the attitudes that can be found in the commercial world.

It is equally important that academics understand the financial drivers of those in the business community with whom they have to deal. Venture capitalists are answerable to their own shareholders, not to the negotiating partners. A major company employee acts for his or her company in agreeing a deal and this must be remembered. So too, and it is helpful to be sufficiently aware, are some of the examples where things have gone wrong with disastrous results.

> **In general universities at last do have coherent policies on intellectual property and in-house professionals to negotiate royalties or equity shares in spin-out companies.**

Having set the scene, we will now turn to experienced practitioners to provide their individual insights.

5. A Judge's View

By The Rt. Hon. Professor Sir Robin Jacob

I n 2007 we had, in the Court of Appeal, a case about the use of computer modelling for the design of rock drill bits.[1] Aspects of the case were potentially very difficult technically, involving as they did some very complicated algorithms and other stuff. So it was agreed the Court should have the assistance of a scientific advisor. Such a person is not a member of the Court and plays no part in the decision: his or her job is to educate the court in the technology (and make sure we don't make any technical gaffs!). The scientific advisor who was appointed was Professor David Limebeer, then of Imperial College[2] and now of Oxford University.[3] As a Judge I had never had the benefit of a scientific advisor before, though Sydney Brenner[4] had acted as such in two cases in which I had appeared as counsel.[5] It is a procedure which works well, and I have used it twice again with much success.[6] The academics all enjoyed it hugely – and found it very instructive. David Limebeer went so far as to invite me to give a lecture about patents to Imperial College. This I did.[7] I found I had a huge audience – Imperial's scientists clearly felt they wanted to know something about patents. A year or so later I volunteered to do a similar exercise at my own alma mater, the Cavendish Laboratory in Cambridge. Again the entirely voluntary turn-out was enormous.[8]

What does this tell you so far? Well, firstly if ever the opportunity of being a scientific advisor to the English Patents Court comes up, seize it with both hands.[9] But more importantly, academic scientists are anxious about patents. They are anxious about a number of things. Firstly, I suppose, they are anxious that somehow the patent system could make, for them or their institution, a great deal of money (stories of professors becoming rich abound – and quite a few are true). Academics don't want to miss out on that but are profoundly uneasy that it depends on things they do not really understand, patent law in particular and the world of business in general. Second, to them, unlike their hard science or engineering, the law is a sort of human-devised complex system – a force which hangs over things without ever being clear or measurable. Thirdly, there is the thought that somehow patent law may interfere with their academic freedom to publish. Fourthly, there may even be a feeling that their institution, particularly in these hard times, would prefer them to research fields which have a real prospect of valuable patents thus compromising their academic freedom to choose their own fields of research. There may even be the worry that money will be allocated to those whose work might lead to valuable patented inventions and away from pure research.

> **" Academic scientists are anxious about patents. "**

I do not say that some of these worries are not justified, for they are. But others can be alleviated if not removed by a better understanding of the patent system and the way it works. I think all academic scientists and engineers should have some education about that. Not a lot, but enough to know when they will need to know more. In industry, researchers will, or should, meet patent attorneys on a regular basis and will have experience of the system. That is less likely for academic researchers.[10]

Before I go on, I think it is well worth standing back to examine the complexities surrounding inventions by academics. A research-based company has much greater clarity. Typically such a company will employ scientists or engineers to find (invent) new or better products or processes. When they do, patents will be applied for to protect the fruits of that research. There is seldom any doubt as to who owns the invention (the basic rule is simple: if you are employed to invent then any invention is your employer's, just as if you are employed to make boots, the boots you make belong to your employer). Nor is there any or much of a problem about the patenting process. The inventor paid for by a company to invent will naturally expect to spend time on patenting his invention. Looking further down, if there is infringement, the claim will be by, and funded by, the employer. If it is to be settled (or damages are awarded) it is all down to the employer. No one else comes into it.

Contrast that paradigm case of an innovative commercial company with that of a university. For a university there will be complexity of ownership of inventions between the academics and the university. The academic scientist is not primarily employed to invent at all, though if he does make an invention he will probably do so in working time and using university-owned facilities and equipment. The law here is not straightforward in practice. The basic rule is that an invention is owned by the inventor(s). But an invention made by an employee

> 'shall, as between him and his employer, be taken to belong to his employer... if (a) it was made in the course of the normal duties of the employee or in the course of duties falling outside his normal duties, but specifically assigned to him, and the circumstances in either case were such that an invention might reasonably be expected to result from the carrying out of his duties; or (b) the invention was made in the course of the duties of the employee and, at the time of making the invention, because of the nature of his duties and the particular responsibilities arising from the nature of his duties he had a special obligation to further the interests of the employer's undertaking.'[11]

Academic scientists are expected to conduct research. So if that research results directly in an invention it seems fairly clear that it will have been made 'in the course of the employee's normal duties'. But things are often more complicated than that. Research may result in new knowledge. But the invention which the academic makes may not be actually part of his research – just an invention made in the light of the research results. There is room for messy dispute here.

Then there is the further complexity introduced because inventions may be made (wholly or in part) by students, particularly research students. Who owns the rights in such inventions? What are the *normal duties* of a research student and was the invention within those duties? The answer is likely to be unclear unless provided for by clear prior agreements.

Yet another problem is the potential for conflict of interest between the academic and his university. His or her interest may well be in maximising his income, possibly at the expense of the university. Thus, for example, he may

❛❛ Academic scientists are expected to conduct research. So if that research results directly in an invention it seems fairly clear that it will have been made 'in the course of the employee's normal duties. ❜❜ have a commercial interest in his research students working on areas which might benefit a spin-off company in which he is involved.

Next is the complexity and tension arising from the academic's need to publish as soon as possible and the basic requirement of patent law that an invention must be novel and non-obvious on the date of filing the patent application: the academic wants to publish at once, his university's attorney says 'wait until I have written a specification to file, a specification which not only contains your idea but enables that ordinary skilled man to work the invention'.

Then there is the cost of patenting. This has two main aspects. First is simply the cost in lost time of the academics. A well-drawn patent specification takes time – both of the attorney who drafts and the inventors themselves. It is an exacting task. So it is all too easy for the academic to get bored and pay insufficient attention – he or she may well feel that they have better things to do such as pressing on with their research, teaching, writing a paper or even marking exams. Inventing is not an academic's primary objective. Still less is checking with care a draft patent specification and, even more importantly, patent claims. One way attention can be improved is if the inventor understands how and in what way the specification and its claims may be used in the future. And there needs to be some fun involved. The patenting process can also be constructive – when it comes to claim drafting the inventors will (or should) always be asked to think of ways round what is claimed. Patenting a new idea can itself result in inventors having more new ideas.[12]

The second aspect of the cost of patenting is money: attorneys' and official fees. Good attorneys and lawyers – especially in the field of IP – are not cheap, but then good advice is seldom cheap. And it seldom pays to do it on the cheap. As to official fees, even though an initial application is cheap, fees can build up quickly from the end of the first year priority period. Decisions have to be made about where patents are to be applied for and appropriate fees paid. Good attorneys can generally delay the points at which commitments have to be made, but there are limits to this. In the nature of things the commercial prospect of an invention is generally difficult to assess at an early stage. So calculated commercial gambles have to be taken – not the sort of thing which comes naturally to universities.

This latter complexity is a reflection of a more general fact. University governance is in the nature of things different from that of a commercial company. Different universities have different structures, but it is fair to say that none of them will have a structure designed for profit or the exploitation of intellectual property. For that reason most, if not all, universities have put systems in place for exploitation of university IP. I will call these systems *exploitation offices*. Exploitation may be carried out in a variety of ways, as I discuss more below, but nearly always it is likely to involve a complex relationship between the commercial exploiter and the university. Exploitation offices have a very difficult job. Such an office is intrinsically an add-on to the university's main function and as such may well be treated by many academics and administrators as peripheral or even a nuisance. Huge commercial nous and legal skills are needed yet these are very hard to come by. The officer must be something of a politician to juggle all the competing interests. Looking in as a lawyer and judge, I have seen some failures here. I will come to some stories later. For the present it is sufficient to note that unless considerable care is taken by the exploitation office a lot can go wrong.

> **“ Unless considerable care is taken by the exploitation office a lot can go wrong. ”**

Before I go on to stories I must discuss copyright. Traditionally universities treated works written by academics as belonging to the author and not the employing university. Yet the Copyright, Designs and Patents Act provides that 'where a literary work is made by an employee in the course of his employment, his employer is the first owner of any copyright in the work subject to any agreement to the contrary'.[13] Traditionally academics have been free to write for themselves not only articles (which seldom if ever make money) but also textbooks. Some of the latter can be profitable indeed. And some universities are beginning to eye big incomes from works written by academics. The suggestion is that these days publication in the field of the academic is really part of his or her job, that part of their employment duties are to write and hence the writing is 'in the course of employment'. Universities can, these days, point to the methods of assessment and funding of universities would take into account publications of the academics: academics are under pressure to publish not merely as a matter of prestige in their own interest but in the interests of their university. Similarly, if an academic were to make a podcast for which he charged for his lectures, the university would say 'you are employed to give the lecture: the copyright in it belongs to us'.

What are the lessons to be drawn from all these complexities? Well there is no complete watertight solution. Perhaps the first lesson to learn is that everyone needs to understand what the complexities are. It is no good academics getting excited and saying 'it should all be ours'. Likewise universities need to operate rationally and fairly. Agreements need to be put in place. People can get frightfully excited even at this stage – before any invention has even been made. There are well-known examples of this, resulting in no clear agreement.

A very important thing for all to understand is that disputes, whether between academics and their university or between a university and a commercial entity, are apt to strangle the commercialisation of an invention anyway with the result that no one makes any or much money. A few years back Southampton University operated a very aggressive IP policy. It led to two lots of litigation (both of which the university lost). One does not matter for present purposes.[14] But the other[15] clearly shows a dispute strangling commercialisation and is an object lesson in the dangers of taking too aggressive a stand.

> **" Disputes are apt to strangle the commercialisation of an invention anyway with the result that no one makes any or much money. "**

The facts were somewhat comic. A university professor had discovered that electrically-charged particles would stick to the joints of cockroaches. A trap using this feature was devised and patented. Some publicity about it was read by an employee of a company which sold magnetically-charged particles. He rang the professor up to suggest that these might work too. The professor said he would try them and was sent a sample of the powder. He got some research workers to see if they worked. And they did. Then the university patented the idea all for itself. Not surprisingly the company complained. The university would not give way, so the company took the dispute to the Patent Office. It decided the invention belonged to the company. The university, surprisingly, appealed to the High Court and had a bit of success in that the judge thought there was a joint invention. The company appealed and we, in the Court of Appeal, decided no: the invention was solely that of the company. During the course of argument (some eight years after the invention had been made) we asked whether there was any commercial exploitation. We were told there had been none. I was not surprised: who would go ahead in the market if he knew that the patent might be awarded to someone else? Actually it is worth my reproducing here some of what I said at the end of my judgement:[16]

> 'I think it is worth making some further observations about entitlement cases in general:
>
> Many disputes of fact are likely to arise – who thought of what and who suggested what to whom are the sort of issues where perceptions after the event are all too likely to differ, people being what they are. It is all too understandable that one man is likely to overestimate his input at the expense of others, even where he is fundamentally honest. Disputes about this sort of issue can readily become overheated and prolix.
>
> Such disputes are all the more likely where the parties' relationship has not been reduced to writing – then complex questions as to implied legal relationships may themselves bedevil the dispute.
>
> Parties to these disputes should realise, that if fully fought, they can be protracted, very, very expensive and emotionally draining. On top of that, very often development or exploitation of the invention under dispute will be stultified by the dead hand of unresolved litigation. That may be the case here: there has not yet been any exploitation by either side, some eight years after the original PCT application. It will often be better to settle early for a smaller share than you think you are entitled to – a small share of large exploitation is better than a large share of none or little.
>
> This sort of dispute is particularly apt for early mediation. Such mediation could well go beyond conventional mediation (where the mediator facilitates a consensual agreement). I have in mind the process called "medarb" where a "mediator" trusted by both sides is given the authority to decide the terms of a binding settlement agreement. Such a power in effect already exists in the Comptroller once he has found a case of entitlement (see s.8(2)). But by then it will probably be far too late.'

I remain of that view. Disputes between academics and their university which are taken to the death about who is right are likely to kill both sides and maybe the invention too. It is better to have an early settlement so that commercialisation can be pressed on with. Note particularly that I favour medarb. You get a neutral in (it will almost certainly have to be a lawyer). In about a day he or she hears all concerned and decides who gets what including percentage shares of profits or royalties. It is all done and dusted – a bit crude but in the end probably everyone will make more money than if it were decided, years down the line, they had a higher percentage (or even the totality) of the rights.

I turn to agreements. From time to time well-meaning but fairly useless documents emerge from government which recommend in general terms that things should be sorted out by way of agreements. Another one has just emerged, 'Intellectual Asset Management for Universities', published[17] by the Patent Office.[18] It contains guidance given at so general a level as to be of little practical use.[19] What would be of much more practical use is a series of examples of agreements – a precedent book – showing the sort of agreement which works for: (a) relationships between full-time academics and their university; (b) students including research students and their university; (c) licensing agreements between the university and commercial companies; (d) spin off agreements and company structures; and (e) collaborative agreements between universities and commercial companies. There may be other sorts of agreement too. I am not suggesting mandatory standard form agreements; I doubt that would work. What is needed are precedents to guide those concerned with producing an agreement for a particular case.

> **❝ It is better to have an early settlement so that commercialisation can be pressed on with. ❞**

Finally I turn to a subject which has not, at least visibly, entered the arena at all – employees' rights to compensation. Under section 40 of the Patents Act 1977 as amended, if an employee has made an invention belonging to his employer for which a patent has been granted he can apply to the Patent Office or the Court for *compensation*. This is to be a *fair share* of the benefit which the employer has derived or may be expected to derive from the invention, patent or the assignment of these.[20] There is little precedent on how this is all supposed to work.[21] The legislation is ill drafted but I think one can fairly say that inventions which have made a lot of money are likely to result in substantial compensation. The section will apply to cases where, as a matter of law, the invention made by the academic belongs to his employer. It does not seem to matter whether it so belongs by operation of law or by reason of an agreement.

Because the principles for compensation are so woolly, this is yet another area suitable for medarb at an early stage. The Shanks case is an example of how prolonged and uncertain things can be if you go down the litigation route with one or both sides taking an extreme position.

Endnotes

[1] *Halliburton v Smith International* [2006] EWCA Civ 1715.

[2] *As Head of the Depar*tment of Electrical and Electronic Engineering and Professor of Control Engineering.

[3] Professorial Fellow of New College and Professor of Control Engineering.

[4] Now Sir Sydney Brenner, a Nobel Laureate and CH.

[5] *Genentech's Patent* [1989] RPC 147 where he sat with the Court of Appeal and *Chiron v Murex Diagnostics* [1996] RPC 535 where he sat both with the judge of first instance (where I appeared) and on appeal (by which time I was on the Bench). The House of Lords in *Kirin-Amgen v Hoechst-Marion Roussel* [2005] RPC 9, also a genetic engineering case, used a scientific advisor, Professor Michael Yudkin of Oxford University to help it understand the technology by way of a series of seminars prior to the hearing.

[6] *Human Genome Sciences v Eli Lilley* [2010] EWCA Civ 33 (currently under appeal to the Supreme Court) where the scientific advisor was Dr John Murphy a Senior Lecturer of the Immunology, Infection and Immunity Research Group within the Division of Life Sciences of King's College London and *Schlumberger v Electromagnetic Geoservices* [2010] RPC 33 where the scientific advisor was Dr Colin Brown, Director of the Ryan Institute for Environmental, Marine and Energy Research at the National University of Ireland, Galway. In both cases the advisor sat with the court in addition to having provided a teach-in prior to the hearing.

[7] The Reeves lecture 2007.

[8] The Director, Peter Littlewood, told me it was one of the biggest for the one-off talks by a guest speaker which the Cavendish lays on Wednesday afternoons for the faculty as a whole.

[9] And make sure you and/or your institution is well paid! The fees lawyers are prepared to pay for a good expert or scientific advisor are higher than most scientists can imagine! Lawyers never charge less than £200 per hour. Partners often come in at £500 an hour or more. A distinguished academic should bear this in mind when setting her fees.

[10] One of the best-run patent departments when I was a young barrister was EMI's – the department was, deliberately, adjacent the main research facility. One of the things the attorneys use to do was just to wander around the research people asking them what they were up to – often a scientist will think that what he is doing is not patentable when it is. Universities may well find that it makes sense to set up something similar rather than relying on their academics to initiate discussions about patentability.

[11] Patents Act 1977 s.39(1)

[12] I remember in a similar but different context a client making an invention whilst considering in what way he wanted to define what a proposed licensee should pay for in a settlement agreement. Before the draft was submitted to the other side a patent application was made so as to cover a possibility the inventor would never have thought of but for the dispute.

[13] Copyright, Designs and Patents Act 1988, s.11(2) re-enacting previous law.

[14] There was a six-day entitlement hearing in the Patent Office – some of the detail is recorded in my judgement in *Schlumberger v EMGS* [2010] WECA Civ 819 at paras. [125]-[127]. It must have cost the University a small fortune.

[15] *IDA v University of Southampton* [2006] ECA Civ 145.

[16] Para. 44

[17] May 2011. It can be found on the Intellectual Property website (**www.ipo.gov.uk**).

[18] Which has an operating name of Intellectual Property Office – the change of name being one of the major achievements of the last but one hastily and ill-constructed reviews of the whole of IP law, the Gowers Review of 2006.

[19] It may be said that this article is at a similar level, but then I am not trying to give much guidance. I am trying to identify the problems.

[20] I paraphrase.

[21] Such as there is consists mainly of a decision to which I was party, *Unilever v Shanks* [2010] EWCA Civ 1283, and a decision of Floyd J, *Kelly v GE* [2009] EWHC 181 (Pat).

6. The Viewpoint of a Patent Attorney

By Ian Bingham

Protecting *art* or Intellectual Property

I t is difficult, in my opinion, to decide whether universities should actively protect intellectual property created by employees. Furthermore, it is even more challenging to decide if universities should strive to commercialise the results of their employees' research. The main function of any academic institution is to focus on research and teaching to increase the intellectual capability of students and then release them as graduates into the unsuspecting world of commercial activity. If we simply do that, however, then we will be failing to equip graduates for the real world and prevent universities from benefitting from their contribution to society as a whole. In one sense, intellectual property is the same as any other form of property, but in the hands of academics it is often *art* in the purest sense and not all art finds a practical application in the real world.

Although I am not an academic and I have not undertaken any pure research, I have sat in wonder when academics have presented their findings and then marvelled at the ingenuity of those able to translate their results of pure research into practical solutions to real problems. The role of a pure academic is finished the moment he or she completes the equation they have been struggling with for years or when they observe the hitherto unknown or unrealised effect that nature has provided. At that point, they have created a form of art that their peers can admire but of which few can appreciate the true significance.

> " **There seems little point in protecting the pure artistic endeavours of any university employee but if one can find a practical application for the stroke of genius behind the artistic expression worthy of commercialisation then that may deserve to be protected.** "

Whilst this creation has arisen as a direct result of the application of an academic's intellect, knowledge and creativity, it does fit the accepted definition of *intellectual property*, even if it is often difficult for the pure academic to appreciate the full significance of what he or she has discovered or realised and how it may change the world. There seems little point in protecting the pure artistic endeavours of any university employee but if one can find a practical application for the stroke of genius behind the artistic expression worthy of commercialisation then that may deserve to be protected. This chapter presents my views in support of universities protecting the intellectual property that finds a comfortable place in the commercial world.

Applying research to the real world

It is not easy to take pure research and find a commercial problem to which it can be applied. Indeed, it often takes a great deal of skill to grasp even the basics of many discoveries, let alone realise how they may be used in the wider world. It could be argued that the role of a pure academic is to redefine the boundaries of human knowledge but, in my view, there is little point or personal gratification in doing that if one does not see the results being put to good use. Whilst many academics seem to be content to concentrate on pure research there are also a growing number of academics who appreciate that there may be a good commercial application for their research and actively participate in helping industry commercialise good science. Whilst this activity is growing, it is still difficult to obtain support from industry for early-stage research as there is no clearly defined commercial outcome. There is, therefore, still a significant obstacle to the application of research in the real world as the commercialisation of research must accommodate the requirements of both the academic and industry.

Whilst it may be hard for an academic to appreciate the commercial aspects of his research it is often more difficult for industry to appreciate the significance of new pure research and how consumers might benefit from the knowledge gained by such research. However, when industry does make the connection great things can happen. Taking an example, it must have been incredibly difficult for industry to appreciate the significance and commercial possibilities behind the science of Magnetic Resonance Imaging discovered and developed by Sir Peter Mansfield et al., but I am sure that all involved are justifiably proud of their contribution to the world whilst also humbled at the success of their own inventions and the direct benefit to mankind of such a wonderful diagnostic tool. The important and growing role in bridging the gap between academia and industry is now undertaken by a University Technology Transfer Manager, as discussed later herein.

The environment and commercial imperatives of industry are very different from those of academia, and, if industry is to survive and prosper, it must protect the inventions that it commercialises. It is this issue that creates much of the friction between academics and industry. Although it is appropriate to challenge the ownership of science (as, for example, referred to by The University of Manchester's Institute for Science Ethics and Innovation in a later chapter), challenging the protection that intellectual property provides for industry is more difficult to justify. This is because large investments are made to translate the results of pure research into commercial products so industry simply must

❝ If universities are to remain at the forefront of innovation and secure their commercial futures then it is appropriate to consider protecting the inventions they make in order to help industry protect the products it manufactures. ❞

protect and develop its competitive position if we are to reap the benefits of their investment. If universities are to remain at the forefront of innovation and secure their commercial futures then it is appropriate to consider protecting the inventions they make in order to help industry protect the products it manufactures.

Attacking the patent system

A recent attack on patenting came from the European Commission when it suggested that patents are anti-competitive and, therefore, bad for the consumer. The EC did seem to fall just short of suggesting they should be banned altogether though. The Commission failed to appreciate the fact that protection provided by a patent gives the investor a limited monopoly sufficient to recover the investment and make a reasonable profit which can return a dividend to the investor and enable capital to be recycled to fund more pure or applied research in the future.

This brings us back to research, much of which is now done by academics, many of whom are funded either partially or wholly by industry. Many academic researchers are, therefore, part of the commercialisation process and are dependent upon the perpetuation of the effective commercialisation of academic research. This dependence means that academics and the universities they work for need to receive remuneration for the research they have done when it is commercialised. The best way to ensure that this remuneration occurs is for the ideas to be protected as they are created – through patents – and for the academics who developed the ideas to work with industry to develop the products that we, the consumers, seek. Any resulting licence income generated as part of a patent arrangement is often free of ties, can be applied by the university for any type of research and may well also help fund pure research that might not otherwise be funded. As well as this, it is only fair that academics should benefit from the commercialisation of their ideas and protecting the IP they create is the way to allow this to happen.

The role of a patent attorney

It seems reasonable to conclude then that it is right to protect the results of academic research by way of a patent or other forms of intellectual property and that is where I, as a patent attorney, make my contribution to the process. It is clear to me that the role of a patent attorney in the process of transferring pure research into commercial reality is an important one as many a commercial opportunity has been missed for want of securing good intellectual property protection.

Patents have different functions and values for different people. I was fortunate enough to have started my career as a Rolls-Royce-sponsored undergraduate where patents were filed to protect the design modifications and improvements to the basic jet engine invented by Sir Frank Whittle. As mentioned in an earlier chapter, the basic principle of jet engines and how to make them was disclosed to the US government as part of the Lend-Lease settlement process after the second world war and the likes of GEC and Pratt & Witney made excellent commercial use of the disclosed information. Whilst Rolls-Royce still became a major player in the global aviation engine market one cannot help wonder what sort of position it would be in if it had been able to exercise the typical 20-year monopoly over the manufacture of the jet engine that a patent provides. The value of the patents would have been immense.

Whilst training as a patent attorney I handled a new but very simple technology aimed at improving the seals along the shaft of a gas turbine engine, thereby improving both the efficiency and power of the engine. This relatively simple technology was much admired by one of the US collaborators in a joint venture in the late 1980s and was licenced in exchange for the solution to a technical problem Rolls-Royce was grappling with, thus saving both time and money and allowing the engine to meet the performance required by the aviation industry.

In that particular instance it would have been easy to calculate the savings made in the project and therefore attribute value to the patents which prevented the collaborator simply copying the relatively simple and easily reproduced idea. Sometimes, however, the valuation of intellectual property is more complex and requires an in-depth knowledge of the market, and the strength and breadth of the patents and other intellectual property in question. Some guidance on how to address these issues is offered later in this chapter.

What makes a good commercial patent?

I am often asked what makes a good commercial patent. I don't have a simple answer to the question as it is not easy to define, but I certainly know a good commercial patent when I see one. I would like to share with you what I look for when reviewing patents and assessing their commercial value.

I have conducted many assessments of patent portfolios and it is clear that one must appreciate both the genius behind the original research and the magnitude of the benefit when enshrined in a potential commercial product. Furthermore, the strength or otherwise of any intellectual property must be considered before one can appreciate the value and power of the patents concerned.

I was once asked to provide an assessment of an extremely large portfolio that had been offered to BTG PLC by a major Japanese manufacturer and settled down to what I thought would be a very lengthy task. Having captured all the patents in electronic form I began to review them and quickly realised that, despite the fact there were some 100 patents or more, they had very little commercial value. They all related to cathode ray tubes and methods of manufacturing them. The scientific literature at the time was full of the new application of LED technology to flat screen displays which came to the market remarkably quickly and completely displaced the old cathode ray tubes. My assessment lasted just ten minutes, five of which were used to pass on the bad news.

> **" One must appreciate both the genius behind the original research and the magnitude of the benefit when enshrined in a potential commercial product. "**

Other technologies and patents are more difficult to assess, particularly when the inventions relate to a technology that is genuinely new to the world. Under these circumstances it is almost pointless doing patent searches to see if anyone might be copying the idea because it is unlikely, although not impossible, that others would also have protected their own similar solutions to the same problem. Academic research based intellectual property is a good example of this as it is close to the point of discovery and therefore unlikely to be being used by others.

Professor Ward and lithium polymer batteries

I am mindful of some of the inventions made by Professor Ian M. Ward, FRS of Leeds University, who is fairly typical of many leading university inventors with a good grasp of the needs of industry and the ability to foresee how science might help. An industrial background at ICI endowed Professor Ward with the industrial and commercial understanding needed to straddle the academic and commercial world. His innovative mind allows him to apply his knowledge to create solutions to problems that many had yet to realise existed. Take, for example, his work in lithium polymer batteries, where he was one of the first to capture the volatile liquid chemical components within a gel material that allowed for the creation of an inherently safe battery. The solvent contained in his gel material functioned above a given temperature but not below and not at the normal operational temperature of the battery. This simple step means that the volatile chemical components such as Lithium can be captured within a gel material during manufacture rather than infused therein after the battery is made.

This is a relatively simple step indeed but it solves the problem of how to successfully mix the chemical components and infuse them into the battery whilst also preventing them escaping in the event of a battery cell being damaged. Furthermore, the invention allows for the rapid extrusion and lamination of gel material with associated electrodes which enhances the cell performance as hot bonding of the gel to the electrode enables electrons to pass across the electrode/gel boundary more easily whilst also enabling the rapid manufacture of cells in the form of a continuous or semi-continuous strip.

The prior art was limited and searching failed to identify anything that could adversely affect the patentability and the two core patent families were granted in all major countries without substantial claim amendment. The patents remained relatively obscure for the best part of ten years until others started working in the area of polymer batteries and then the patent landscape suddenly exploded.

Only then could the significance of the inventions and their impact on the manufacture of a product that we all use on a daily basis be appreciated. Professor Ward and his team had created some fundamental patents in an emerging technology which were likely to become extremely valuable. With the rise in hybrid vehicles, the market for lithium polymer batteries is likely to become enormous and these patents may well become equally valuable but it would have taken an exceptionally forward-thinking person to have realised this at the start of the inventive and patenting process.

Maximising the commercial value of a patent

Maximising the commercial value of a patent requires more than just capturing the inventive concept described to the attorney. A good patent draft goes much further and considers future value – the role of the attorney is of paramount importance in this process.

The primary function of a patent attorney is to protect the invention described and the product that will be manufactured by the client. To do more exposes the patent application to greater scrutiny during search and examination and may well cause the application to fail. The real commercial value that can be realised through the application of the inventive concept may not lie in the invention itself and it is this value that needs to be captured if the resulting patents are to be of high commercial value.

> **❝ The primary function of a patent attorney is to protect the invention described and the product that will be manufactured by the client. ❞**

To capture this value one must push the boundaries and explore the inventive concept and how it will be utilised and build the additional knowledge into the patent application, but at the same time keeping in mind that the more one discloses, the greater the likelihood that the examiner might discover some relevant prior art. The task is, admittedly, a difficult one, but can be extremely rewarding.

John Bissler and improved haemofiltration

An instructive example is the invention by a medical researcher and clinical practitioner John Bissler, MD, of Cincinnati Children's Hospital, relating to haemofiltration, which is a technique used to filter a patient's blood and remove excretory substances that would otherwise be removed by the kidneys. Early machines were extremely difficult to operate, inaccurate, and required intensive monitoring of the patient and continuous manual intervention in their operation. This was problematic, particularly in a busy intensive care ward or when the machines are used on neo-natal patients with extremely small blood volumes.

Dr. Bissler developed a control system that could ensure that, according to Claim 1, '*a pre-selected amount of fluid was removed in a pre-selected period of time*' and in one step released the intensive care staff from a very time-consuming task whilst ensuring each patient was safely and appropriately treated. This was a fundamental improvement over older machines and the approach was adopted by a number of the leading manufacturers who sold haemofiltration machines, disposable filters and the replacement fluids that were prescribed for the patient and which were delivered by the machine itself as part of the dialysis treatment.

Although machines sold for some $20,000 or more and a royalty on the sales would attract a reasonable income, the real commercial value to the manufacturers was in the sale of the disposable filter elements and consumable fluids used to treat the patient, which were delivered as part of the treatment process. The total value of the disposable filters sold each year in association with each machine amounted to approximately $75,000 (estimated) or some $375,000 over the typical lifetime of the machine. The profit associated with the sale of such machines is likely to be less than $2000, whilst the profit associated with the sale of the filters alone was likely to be in excess of $200,000. The value and profit associated with the sale of consumable fluids was not calculated but is likely to be well in excess of that of the disposable filters.

On licensing the technology to the key players in the medical field the big issue revolved around what royalty should be paid and what products should be covered by the royalty payments. Initial acceptance of a royalty on the machines was followed by rejection of any contemplation of a royalty on the disposable filters or indeed the consumable fluids. During the ensuing discussions it was highlighted that Claim 2 was directed to a combination of the innovative machine of Claim 1 and a filter which was used in the process of filtration and which would be disposed of after each patient's treatment. In essence, it was arguable that each time a new filter was placed on the machine and the machine used that a new infringement took place.

After much debate a royalty based on the sale of both machines and the disposable filters was agreed and it is likely that the amount of royalty received was greatly enhanced by the claim covering the disposable filter. The drafting attorney had done an excellent job and at least doubled the value of the patent by the inclusion of the filter in the claim, but the attorney had only been able to do so after fully understanding the totality of the commercial opportunity that would be created as a result of adoption of the invention adequately protected by Claim 1. The expansion of the claims to cover the filters would also have widened the prior art search and may have identified additional prior art which might have prejudiced Claim 1, but the outcome clearly justified the approach.

The above example helps illustrate that industry sometimes fails to provide fully workable solutions to technical problems and that finding a more complete solution to a problem can often greatly enhance commercial opportunity. Often, it is the users of new products that are best placed to appreciate the failings of an existing product and how that may be solved and a patent protecting the solution to the problem can have great value. It also illustrates that the attorney drafting any patent to the new solution needs to be able to appreciate the commercial aspects of the product and draft the claims accordingly in order to protect the full commercial opportunity.

Bundling patents

Whilst the example of Professor Bissler and haemofiltration illustrates the value that can be captured in a patent, it is relatively rare that an actual commercial value for an individual patent can be easily calculated. Indeed, the real value often arises when patents are bundled together as the real value is in the power that control over such a large portfolio gives.

An excellent example is that associated with Magnetic Resonance Imaging (MRI), which is now commonplace in many modern hospitals and has been used to save many a life. Sir Peter Mansfield, Emeritus Professor of Physics at the University of Nottingham and joint winner of the Nobel Prize for Medicine, October 2003, is correctly accredited as being the father of MRI, but many others worked on the technology and many worked on capturing and releasing the commercial value by licensing to the key players in the medical field.

The British Technology Group (BTG, formally The National Research and Development Corporation) were instrumental in coordinating the patenting and technical efforts of experts from the Universities of Oxford, Aberdeen and Nottingham, and efforts with the industrial partner, Oxford Instruments, which developed the wide-bore, high field magnets necessary to perform the imaging. The value captured within the universities and industry – and the value in the patents which protected the commercial position – was greatly enhanced by the fact that it was all available from one licensor, namely BTG, and because a strong patent thicket had been created.

Commercial negotiations with Johnson & Johnson resulted in the first of many patent licences but payments under the licence were withheld and litigation was necessary to ensure the continuing security of the licence income. Litigation was terminated after receipt of agreeable settlement terms which acknowledged the value and validity of the patents and this was instrumental in the successful licensing of the technology to all subsequent licensees. It is estimated that some 99% of all MRI machines produced are made by licensees paying royalties under the agreements negotiated by BTG and in excess of £200 million is thought to have been received in royalty payments, much of which has been returned to the universities and inventors who made it all possible.

It is doubtful that individual inventors and individual universities would have been able to develop the technology to the extent that the group as a whole managed and extremely unlikely that licensing would have been successful without connecting the patents and expertise together and managing the development of the technology in a co-ordinated and commercially appropriate manner. The success of MRI owes much to the foresight of both inventors and commercially minded individuals and the creation of a multi-disciplinary team which worked together towards a common goal.

Strong patent drafting

The patents for each of the technologies mentioned above went well beyond the original invention and captured real and additional commercial value. Before any patent can do this, each patent application must comply with basic requirements of the patent system if it is to be considered to be both strong and broad in scope and avoid being dismissed by industry.

The main issue is one of support in the description of the breadth of claims that the patent attorney has drafted as poorly supported claims may be subjected to amendment during prosecution and valuable claim breadth may be lost for the want of the required support. The European patent Convention, for example, requires that 'the claims shall be supported by the description' (Art. 85 EPC).

Interpretation of this requirement by the European Patent Office is enshrined in The Guidelines for Examination of a European Patent, which is used by examiners during the examination process and provides an explanation of what degree of support is required. In essence, if the claims extend to a range of parameters, such as operational temperatures or pressures for an industrial process, then the main body of the specification must include examples stretching across the entire range claimed. No longer is it appropriate to have a small number of examples within the description as to do so would fail to meet the requirements of support. So, whilst most initial patent applications are filed with very little support for the entire range over which the invention may be applied, this defect can and must be corrected within the first year of filing (convention year) if the full commercial value is to be captured and the breadth of the claims are to be maintained.

Although universities are well placed to explore the boundaries of the ranges claimed and gather the required data there is often a mismatch between the timescales of the patent system and those within which academics are used to operating. A PhD thesis based on exploring the boundaries of the invention is unlikely to be completed within one year of the patent application being filed so great care must be taken with the timing of patent filings and subsequent research programmes. Consequently, any research required to support the claims must be completed well within a 12-month period after filing the initial application so as to allow the attorney time to include it in any subsequently filed patent applications, which must be filed within 12 months of the original application if one is to preserve the filing date of the initial application as the priority date abroad. Securing this priority date can be crucial to preventing others from securing a patent for the same invention in a foreign country if they file an application after the initial application is filed but before you file applications abroad.

The almost impossible task of a university technology transfer manager

Many universities now have their own intellectual property or technology transfer departments which strive to protect and commercialise the inventions arising within the university. Although some research may be aimed at meeting present or near-future needs of industry, meaning it can be more easily evaluated and patent expenditure justified, it is difficult to assess the commercial value of some pure research and decide how to protect it.

The task of a technology transfer officer in a university is difficult owing to the financial constraints they must operate under if they are to protect the bulk of the inventions being created and, by association, the attorney is therefore placed under a great deal of pressure to file an application at reduced cost. Whilst keeping costs down must always be a major consideration in the drafting of a patent application, one must bear in mind that a well-drafted initial application (and an acceptance of the cost concomitant with this) will, generally, help reduce costs in the long run as there will be far fewer mistakes to correct and omissions to include at the end of the convention period. A mistake, undetected error or omission in a patent application is notoriously difficult and sometimes impossible to correct during examination and may lay the application open to attack, so it is far preferable to protect against these errors by drafting the application well initially.

> **" A mistake, undetected error or omission in a patent application is notoriously difficult and sometimes impossible to correct during examination and may lay the application open to attack. "**

Drafting costs can be reduced to a minimum by good presentation of information to the attorney and by clarity of thought before the initial draft is undertaken. A PhD thesis, whilst being extremely valuable and informative, does not form the basis of a good patent application as it is focused on presenting the story of development and discovery rather than the essence and significance of the invention. Therefore, just including large portions of a PhD thesis in a patent application to support the invention may well supply the desired support for the breadth of the claims but it will also significantly increase the length of the patent application and the subsequent translation costs may be prohibitive.

The European Patent Office favours having a *problem-solution* approach to defining an invention in which one must first identify the closest prior attempt at addressing the issue at hand and identify a problem associated with that approach before identifying the specific solution that you have come up with. Whilst this has some inherent problems it can form the basis of a useful starting point when trying to decide where the invention lies and may well help reduce the drafting costs. A good technology transfer officer is able to define the problem to be solved and succinctly describe the solution and present the information in a concise and clear manner to the attorney tasked with protecting the idea. Employing the *problem-solution* approach may well help this process.

Measuring success in the technology transfer sector

It is clear that there has been a significant improvement in the way most university technology transfer operations work but it is virtually impossible to quantify the improvement in any meaningful way. This is because technology transfer is an extremely difficult task in its own right and it is impossible to conclude that failure to commercialise a technology is due solely to lack of effort of the technology transfer team. Indeed, the more commercial an invention is the less effort one would expect to be used in taking it to market.

Various initiatives have measured the number of patents filed or the number of spin-out companies formed. However, the issue with these metrics is that they do not take account of meaningful commercial outcomes such as patents granted and companies funded. Even these are inadequate measures because the gestation period spanning invention, funding, innovation and product development is so long that it is hard to attribute *success* to discrete activities such as patent filing unless or until a deal in which that patent features is executed.

Nonetheless, against this backdrop there are some notable successes. Imperial Innovations is a listed company with a share price to rival that of certain pharmaceutical companies. The University of Strathclyde continues its tradition of rapidly converting concepts into applied science based on a history of working successfully with industrial partners. The Universities of Manchester, Dundee, Nottingham, Oxford and Cambridge have been progenitors of successful spin-out companies and, in more recent years, science parks housing more spin-outs. These new companies have attracted venture capital and local development agency funding, resulting in jobs and the rise of a generation of entrepreneurial company managers.

The Medical Research Council (MRC) and the Wellcome Trust occupy strong positions in the UK technology transfer arena. The Medical Research Council has an enviable track record in technology transfer going back to 1990. The

Wellcome Trust is recognised internationally as a centre of excellence for the development of new medical treatments and supports innovation with generous grant support and investments. In addition, Cancer Research UK has capitalised on its early-stage drug development capability and has initiated a number of innovative industrial partnerships.

In the UK, with nearly 120 universities and about 160 other higher education institutions, these positive examples are the exceptions. Whilst company creation is often seen as the most worthwhile technology transfer endeavour, the fact is that very little of the early-stage intellectual property generated within the university sector is developed enough to support a company. Thus, ultimately, the challenge facing university technology transfer is to identify the strengths of all the intellectual capital at its disposal and to deploy it gainfully.

The focus on patents created and companies formed does not necessarily play to these strengths either. Many universities adopt a strategy by which they must find a licensee within 12 to 18 months of patent filing in the hope that nationalisation costs will be met by that licensee. Patent filing, however, creates intense early timeline pressures that do not sit comfortably alongside the tempo of academic life. In addition, the data requirements for patenting may not align well with more esoteric and arguably intellectually fulfilling research. The need for academic publication flies in the face of the industrial concept of confidentiality. Ultimately, value creation from intellectual property comes not from an invention itself

> **" A better measure of success might be the number of patents filed by the companies formed by the universities rather than by the university itself. "**

but from the innovation that harvests the invention to generate a product of use to a consumer. Consequently, a better measure of success might be the number of patents filed by the companies formed by the universities rather than by the university itself.

Putting a value on the IP

In July 1995, Amgen Inc. (California, US) paid $20 million in upfront fees for exclusive commercial rights under Rockefeller University's obesity gene patent. The deal contained provisions for a reputed $80 million in downstream milestone payments if the gene product, a hormone called leptin, proved effective in combating human obesity. At the time there were estimated to be about 50 million overweight and obese people in the US (there are now reported to be 20 million overweight and obese people in the US) suggesting that this is a highly valuable gene patent and, for Amgen, a timely licence deal. Amgen's share price rose by $4.37 to $84.25 in a single day's trading following the announcement of the deal and, thereby, illustrated the potential value that the market attributed to the possession of the patents by the right party.

There is no doubt that these numbers represent a lot of value, but this deal skewed the notion of the value of gene patents for a long time afterwards. The so-called obesity gene directly encoded a product, leptin, but a lot more development would be needed just to determine if the obesity gene product would reproduce the results in humans that had only been seen in obese mice up to that point. Moreover, other genes do not encode active drug-like proteins but rather the targets for either such proteins or pharmaceuticals. In these cases, the gene patent can only protect the gene and its product; it cannot protect the drugs that are developed to interact pharmacologically with the gene product. Commercially speaking the value lies more in the drug than in its target. This has not stopped an enormous amount of gene patenting and the value of doing this is, at best, moot.

> **"There is a strong argument that universities and higher education/research institutes harbour more value in the form of know-how than they do in their patent estates."**

This is not to say that universities should not and cannot generate value and create platforms for successful innovation and, indeed, the MRI story discussed above illustrates that this can be extremely successful. There is a strong argument, however, that universities and higher education/research institutes harbour more value in the form of know-how than they do in their patent estates. Companies traditionally come to universities when confronted with a gap in their technical arsenal and institutions with the right technology at the right time are well-placed to capitalise (and with some significant lack of risk) by collaborating with companies. Two examples of how universities can capitalise on this other major form of intellectual property are presented below.

Patents versus know-how

In the mid-1990s, it was already apparent that the genomics revolution presented an unexpected paradox. The enormous amount of DNA sequence data being generated was not in fact casting much light on the causes of disease. SmithKline Beecham was an early adopter of gene technology and triggered a massive follow-on from a host of other pharmaceutical companies. The realisation soon dawned, however, that deciphering the genetic code was not enough in itself. The value-creating event was in deciphering the genetic code with respect to disease. Given that at the time it was estimated that the human genome contained some 100,000 genes (now known to be closer to 23,000 protein coding genes) the challenge was in taking a given gene sequence and aligning it with a target disease.

SmithKline Beecham (now GSK) conceived a project that turned the gene paradigm on its head. Instead of starting with gene sequences and working towards disease, they contacted the Medical Research Council (MRC) whose mammalian genetics unit at Harwell in Oxfordshire had developed world-class expertise in the study of human disease using the mouse as a model organism. The mouse, deemed as a good genetic model, offered the opportunity to track back from defects in neuromuscular behaviour to changes in genes (mutations) which might provide the crucial key to understanding disease. The MRC held valuable know-how in the form of a deep understanding of how the mouse physiology (phenotype) and genome (genotype) were connected. A deal was signed in the absence of any patents for a substantial seven-figure sum. The pharmaceutical company paid handsomely for an exclusive three-year option on any intellectual property developed in the course of a programme it had paid for. Within the three years a gene was discovered in relation to a particular defect and it was decided that the MRC should form a know-how company.

Organon BV

The power of genomics lies in the possibility of attributing certain disease traits or the propensity for disease to identified human genes. In the field of mental health the interplay of many genes and complex non-gene cues such as environment and behaviour makes for a particularly challenging situation. The MRC's human genetics unit in Edinburgh had been closing in on genes implicated in bipolar depression and psychoactive disorders for nearly six years when Organon (now part of Pfizer) made contact directly with the principal investigator and offered to provide financial support for the ongoing project in return for access to the IP.

The MRC's value to the pharmaceutical company was in the know-how that it held at that point in time. It was believed that no other research group in the world was so close to identifying new genes implicated in two such major mental illnesses. Moreover, Organon did not have an in-house capability in this area.

A deal was struck in which the research was supported by Organon to the tune of over £1 million. The pharmaceutical company was granted an exclusive option to acquire a licence to any intellectual property rights (IPRs) generated by the MRC as a consequence of the research. Whilst the financial terms were a focus of great effort during the contract negotiations (this deal supported seven academic posts for three years), the most intense negotiation revolved around publication. This became a potential deal-breaker.

The collision between the prerogatives of industry and academia came right to the fore. For three of the senior post doctorate fellows working on the programme, there was the prospect of ground-breaking, quite literally front-page news and possibly career-making publications upon the final identification of the genes. For the drug company, there was a need for an embargo on publication in line with patenting procedures. The MRC resolved the matter by introducing a new concept into the agreement namely, *Fields of Publication*. This is analogous to the *Fields of Use* concept more commonly applied to the permitted use of information divulged in a Confidential Disclosure Agreement (CDA) or the activity for which intellectual property rights might be granted under a patent licence. For the MRC scientists the major story was the identification and mapping of new genes; for Organon, the central issue was to control disclosures relating to new chemical entities (NCEs) that might be patentable. The parties agreed the basis of an Academic Field of Publication and a Commercial Field of Publication.

Final thoughts

If universities are to continue to train the scientists of the future and to redefine the boundaries of science and knowledge to benefit people they must continue to collaborate with industry and protect the intellectual property so crucial to the success of a commercial product. In doing so, they must strive to focus on the creation of commercially-focused intellectual property and protect it by way of both patents and the capture and dissemination of the associated expertise.

7. Technology Transfer Office: The Next Step

By Patricia Barclay

The technology transfer office (TTO) is now an established part of the academic landscape. Different offices may have different focuses – for example Brunel tries to pick *winners* and then put all its professional effort behind a select few projects while Edinburgh, on the other hand, tends to put more limited resources behind a wider range of proposals, allowing the market finally to decide.

For some universities, supporting student inventions is considered important as part of the broader learning mission of the university, while others look more to projects that will create jobs within their community. Yet other universities, following the Glasgow *Easy IP* model, are introducing schemes to make the availability of university technology more widely known and to introduce simple first-step licences. They hope that this will encourage the licensing of technologies that may have been overlooked or tempt companies that are less familiar with the licensing process to take those initial tentative steps to exploring the potential for academic collaborations.

For still other universities the focus is on offering services and engaging with industry by providing additional research capability to local companies, in particular to smaller companies, who may find it more difficult to access particular expertise or may lack the facilities to run particular tests or projects.

To meet these varied goals the staff within TTOs are becoming ever-more professional. Some are recruited directly from business development roles in industry while others come from a more academic background and are then offered specialist training. Organisations such as Praxis Unico in the UK offer high-quality training in relevant skills and provide opportunities through conferences and newsletters for best practice and new ideas to be shared.

Most universities offer courses across an extraordinary range of activities and it would be unreasonable to expect even the largest and most professional TTO to have specific expertise in every relevant industry. This is sometimes seen as a problem as different industries have different risk profiles and flashpoints and so ideally licensing or funding contracts should be drafted with these issues in mind. One solution is reflected in the trend for groups of universities to work together so that expertise in particular fields can be shared and smaller universities can take advantage of the greater resources of their larger neighbours. Such collaborations also allow ideas developed within one institution to be more widely disseminated through cooperative activity in industry showcases and similar initiatives.

> **❝ Universities offer courses across an extraordinary range of activities and it would be unreasonable to expect even the largest and most professional TTO to have specific expertise in every relevant industry. ❞**

Even the best-run TTO can improve its offering and many offices are full of ideas that they would dearly love to put into practice if only they had the time and resources. In this short article I would like to focus upon just three main areas in which there would be clear benefits in the TTO taking the lead to improve practice and which would not necessarily require significant investment:

- Dealing with the unusual collaboration;

- Handling complaints from industrial collaborators; and

- Providing entrepreneurial training.

1. Dealing with the unusual collaboration

TTOs have set procedures for dealing with consultancy services offered by academics, licensing of university technology and establishing spin-out companies. While views may differ on the terms offered by particular universities and the efficiency of their processes, these procedures are generally well understood and handled in a predictable manner. Difficulties arise, however, when the situation is not typical, for example where technologies from several institutions must be included in a licence for the commercialisation project to be viable or where technology has been brought into the institution by a new member of staff.

Where several institutions have got together to develop technology as part of an ongoing formal collaboration there will usually be a contract between them which will set out the rules and procedures for any subsequent commercialisation. Where the funding is part of an international grant though this is not always the case; often there is only a general statement about access to the results. In these cases it would be preferable if an additional document were drawn up between the parties outlining the specific process to be taken with respect to intellectual property protection and exploitation at the beginning of the collaboration.

Regrettably this does not always happen and it may be the case that only after one of the parties has become involved in some type of commercialisation that retrospective activity with all the obvious complications is initiated. This oversight can occur initially because the TTO, which might normally generate an appropriate contract, is simply unaware of the existence of this primarily academic collaboration. The problem could be avoided if the TTO were to educate the finance group responsible for obtaining this type of funding of the potential issues and to offer to provide the additional contract.

Another increasingly common situation is where academics who were not originally working together meet up, perhaps at a conference, and see an opportunity to bring their technologies together in a commercial venture. They then have to deal with two different TTOs who may have conflicting policies and goals and this can lead to very lengthy negotiations which may then be further complicated by the lawyers for all parties doing their best to protect their clients' interests as they perceive them. There is no easy answer to this although it will undoubtedly become an increasing problem as academics become ever more interested in commercialising their ideas and ever more aware of colleagues' activities in other institutions. Perhaps a willingness to forgo their own preferred terms in favour of a more generic form, say along the lines of the Lambert agreements might provide a way forward. (**www.ipo.gov.uk/lambert**)

Academics are becoming increasingly mobile and will inevitably seek to commercialise ideas later in their careers that first began to crystallise some years before when they were either students or employed by another organisation (which may or may not have been an academic institution). The first issue of course is to sort out who owns what and to ensure that no previous employer or financing organisation has a prior claim on the technology, but what happens then? Where the TTO of the new institution the academic has recently joined is providing services to support the commercialisation activities of the new academic it does not seem unreasonable that the institution should be in some way compensated for that support, however it seems wholly inequitable that that compensation should be the same whether the technology is brought in from outside or whether it is developed within and owned by that university.

The new academic may feel in a poor bargaining position here – they are new in the post, perhaps anxious for their position and unfamiliar with the culture and processes of the new organisation – and so they may feel that they have no alternative but to go along with whatever is proposed by the university. In the long term of course this may well lead to a growing resentment, a sense of having been cheated by the university and to a dissatisfied and unsettled employee.

This could be avoided were the university to set out a policy for dealing with circumstances of this nature which recognised the difference in this situation from one where the technology was internally developed. Clear guidelines could also be given to the TTO on how such a deal should be structured. An appropriate starting point might be the terms used for student inventions at many universities, whereby the university will provide minimal support and the student maintains all their rights, or if the student requests the university will provide more substantial support in return for a share of the ultimate rewards.

2. Handling complaints from industrial collaborators

Most relations between academia and industry move along relatively smoothly with any minor hiccoughs that are encountered being resolved between those most directly involved. Sometimes the situation can become a little more heated but again negotiation between the more senior officers of the organisation and the more senior academics in the relevant department can generally sort things out. Sadly, however, some projects do go seriously awry and academic institutions do not always handle these problems effectively.

Let us look at two recent case studies.

The Multitasking Academic and the Pontius Pilate of the TTO

In the first situation an academic entered into a commercialisation collaboration with a multinational industrial partner leading to the establishment of a spin-out company. The research moved slowly and the industrial partner became caught up in an internal reorganisation and was not closely involved in the project for some time before finally announcing that it did not wish to continue the collaboration. The academic found an alternative investor who bought out the industrial partner. The new investor failed to undertake any detailed due diligence but relied on the reputation of the university and the fact that a large company had previously been involved.

Fairly rapidly the relationship began to deteriorate; the investor found it difficult to arrange meetings with the academic or to obtain detailed reports on the scientific activity being undertaken. He became concerned as to whether the funds he was investing in the project were being used appropriately and with difficulty obtained some limited information on the expenditure which seemed to suggest that project funds were being used for purposes external to the project, including extensive foreign travel. Being unable to obtain any detailed information from the academic partner he reverted to the TTO who had been involved in setting up the collaboration.

The TTO was in a difficult position as it had no direct authority over the academic or access to much of the relevant material. After putting up a number of unconvincing and contradictory arguments, such as that monies given to the academic were intended as a gift which he could use as he wished, the institution did eventually agree to a limited settlement with respect to some portion of the misused funds. This did not resolve the whole problem however as the investor alleged that the academic had breached the terms of confidentiality with respect to the spin-out's technologies and he had still not been granted access to the data produced by the academic and his group within the university on behalf of the spin-out.

The situation was highly complex as the academic was a shareholder and director of the spin-out, a consultant to the spin-out under a separate contract and the chief investigator under a contract with his academic institution to conduct the principal R&D activities of the company: each contract contained confidentiality provisions, so which contract had he breached?

The university took the view that any breach was by the academic personally under the consultancy agreement and so it was not their responsibility. They were also reluctant to share the data produced under the research contract for the spin-out company; their claims ranged from the company not being entitled to the data, to it already having been handed over, to its simply not being available. The TTO claimed that any dispute regarding the conduct of the research agreement should not be taken up with them but with the head of the relevant academic department.

It is unclear to what extent the head of this department examined the claims in detail as the investigation, if indeed one were conducted, was entirely confidential to the university with no details being shared with the investor, who naturally felt poorly treated and suspicious of the findings. The investor also made allegations regarding a publication which he claimed had been made contrary to the terms of the research agreement and that which in any case contained incorrect data, a position supported by one of the co-authors. The TTO again stated that this was not something with which they could involve themselves and instead referred the investor to another procedure – this time for academic misconduct. The investor followed this but again all the hearings and discussions were internal and he was given no information as to the substance of the defence. He learned that no evidence was taken from the co-author. Unsurprisingly he was rather cynical when told, at the conclusion of the process, that there was no case to answer and that the co-author was mistaken and a less able researcher.

Lessons from this case study

How might this have been handled more effectively? Firstly, of course, the investor should have conducted detailed due diligence and taken action more swiftly when problems arose. This is likely to be a growing problem as it is an increasingly widespread practice for redundant executives who may be inexperienced in this aspect of business to invest in start-up companies. It is not really the TTO's concern to tell investors how to run their businesses but they may wish to prepare a due diligence package which may at least prevent some misunderstandings later. A huge problem with this particular project were the multiple hats being worn by the academic, which meant it was really difficult to assign liability at any stage. US institutions avoid this by prohibiting an academic from taking on these multiple roles. UK institutions might also look at how this could be addressed.

It is inevitable that unhappy investors or industrial partners will first look to the TTO to resolve any problems. In many cases the TTO will be their principal contact with the institution other than the academic with whom they have fallen out – indeed they may have been initially introduced to the academic or the project through the TTO. The TTO is then faced with a situation in which they are normally powerless; they are on the frontline with an increasingly angry partner but they cannot call the academic to account nor can they force disclosure of information even though it may be clearly required by the contract that they themselves have produced. Heads of department are a potential arbiter here but they may have little reason to become actively involved in resolving issues relating to colleague's commercialisation activities. They may be generally interested in maintaining investment in their department but if it is all linked to a particular colleague's project they may see little direct benefit in becoming involved. They may indeed not see the commercialisation activity as any of their business or worse may see it as a

❝ Academic institutions often keep poor scientific and financial records compared with the expectations of industry. It would help if the format for these records and a system for their regular transmission were formally established as this would be beneficial to both parties. ❞

distraction from the department's overall objectives.

Another common problem, and one that occurred in this example, is that academic institutions often keep poor scientific and financial records compared with the expectations of industry. It would help if the format for these records and a system for their regular transmission were formally established as this would be beneficial to both parties – such an arrangement should be included in standard contracts for third-party funded research.

Where an investor or collaborator is receiving regular copies of the data being generated they can see for themselves if the research is progressing appropriately and how the funding is being spent. This would allow them to take up any concerns at an early stage and would make it much easier for any investigation that were necessary to proceed quickly and transparently.

If all investigations are conducted internally without any access to the proceedings by the complainant it is to be expected that he will not be convinced by the outcome. Designing an alternative system and in particular one that can handle all types of complaint through one entry point would go a long way to building confidence in the commitment of the academic institution to the collaboration.

The Invisible Data

The second case study involves a recently retired academic who sought to commercialise research developed in his previous employment. Much of the ongoing research was to be conducted by a younger colleague who was still at the institution and contracts were drawn up by a lawyer acting for the institution. The retired professor, trusting both the institution and their agents, did not himself engage an independent legal advisor. Initially things appeared to be going very well and the research results were spectacular. On the basis of the reported results the professor was able to raise substantial private and public funding to continue the work. The next round of funding was to come largely from institutional investors and with promises of this funding in place the professor requested that the raw data be made available for these prospective investors to undertake their due diligence.

In the meantime, for regulatory purposes, key studies had to be repeated at an independent laboratory. Although the younger colleague who had supervised the work at the institution was engaged as a consultant for these repeat studies his earlier results could not be replicated. At this point he also refused to make this earlier raw data available for due diligence, claiming that the professor and his company had no right to access the material. A long and costly legal process then ensued and finally incomplete records were presented to the retired professor which did not appear to support the claims made either in the reports that were used with the investors or in the patents which had been filed.

The institution, which had subsequently been reorganised and absorbed into a larger organisation, refused to engage in discussion. They claimed the data belonged to the academic notwithstanding both the terms of his employment and the contract with the retired professor's company and referred all matters to their lawyer, the same individual who had drawn up the original agreements.

In both these case studies we can see how matters could have been handled better. The investor/collaborator should have engaged in more detailed due diligence, better contracts should have been drawn up (although to be fair in the first case study the investor used a very well known multinational law firm) and considerable costs could have been avoided had clear and transparent complaints procedures been in place.

Improving contracts

As regards the contracts there is much that could be done to minimise disputes:

- Introduce a clause setting out how a project is to be financed and providing for regular financial reports to the industrial partner, with a right to audit.

- Provide for an agreed form of scientific record keeping for the project with regular delivery of copies of the raw data to the partner together with any reports that are required, again allowing for audit.

- Provide for regular project meetings either physically or by telephone as part of the contractual arrangement itself.

- Educate the academic and his superior on the expectations of the partner under the contract and ensure that they have bought into these obligations before the collaboration starts.

- Consider with care the dispute resolution clause within the contract and ensure that it is appropriate for the situation and is likely to provide a prompt, cost-effective and transparent resolution of the dispute. It is not acceptable to sit back and wait to be sued confident that many companies will not go to this expense or in the case of smaller companies may be unable to afford to seek recompense. While this may stave off trouble in the short-term, word will eventually spread that the institution is a poor partner that does not stand behind its contracts.

Dispute resolution

In researching this article it was difficult to engage with TTOs and find out how they resolve complaints that are brought to them, although there is clearly also some dissatisfaction with the process on their part. Some universities have developed complaints procedures primarily to address the concerns of unhappy students as opposed to industrial partners, but even where they exist it seems that TTOs are unfamiliar with them. I have never seen reference to a formal complaints procedure as part of a contractual dispute resolution clause and yet anecdotally it seems that where they exist and are used they can effectively resolve matters swiftly and in confidence. There would clearly be merit in exploring this option provided that it is both fair and transparent to all concerned.

Another form of dispute resolution that seems particularly well-suited to resolving this type of dispute is mediation, whereby all the parties concerned sit down with a trained neutral to find a way forward that is acceptable to all of them. In mediation the outcome is not limited to damages or injunctive relief but can be more or less whatever the parties feel is most appropriate to their situation. In many collaborations this will be a renegotiation of the contract or the processes under which they are working to something that better meets their needs. It is entirely private, can be

> **[A] form of dispute resolution that seems particularly well-suited to resolving this type of dispute is mediation, whereby all the parties concerned sit down with a trained neutral to find a way forward that is acceptable to all of them.**

arranged within a couple of weeks and is usually concluded within a day so avoiding delays to the research, the build-up of resentment and the entrenchment of positions that can make later resolution so difficult.

3. Providing entrepreneurial training

The final area that I would like to discuss is the manner in which universities attempt to prepare students to take forward their ideas commercially.

A variety of different options have been tried here. Some universities permit students to take a limited number of academic courses outside their core area of study. While for some this may be a way of exploring different topics before they finally make up their mind in which area to specialise, it also provides an opportunity to take complementary courses in support of their final career plans. More specifically designed for life skills, a range of voluntary workshops may be offered to all students across the university. Take-up can be mixed with some students seemingly reluctant to attend activities away from their own faculty buildings while for others there may be issues of marketing with details of relevant courses not necessarily reaching those who would most benefit from attendance.

Entrepreneurs' clubs have commonly been set up and offer a range of activities from pitching competitions to lectures from successful businesspeople. These tend to be enjoyed by the participants but the advice is often focused on either getting started through developing a business plan, presentational skills and ad hoc tips from a chosen speaker rather than systematic support for specific businesses.

Where funding is available intensive workshops over a number of days aiming to provide students with a range of skills necessary for setting up and running a business have been held. As these courses and events are generally voluntary participants are necessarily self-selecting and so it is difficult to obtain reliable data as to the effectiveness of the different schemes. The data that has been put together, in Pecs for example, where intensive business skills workshops have been conducted for some years, does seem to provide evidence that those who attend such courses tend to obtain better paid jobs and faster promotion and are more likely to set up a business than those who do not.

Talking to individuals who have attended different forms of entrepreneurship education and in particular those who have gone on to set up businesses, there do seem to be some common themes, although this discussion is drawn purely upon anecdotal feedback rather than systematic research. There is a distinct preference for being taught along with those from similar backgrounds, so for example bioscience students prefer to take part in classes designed specifically for bioscience students with others from the same faculty rather than attend classes designed to accommodate students from all faculties across the university.

Participation by students from other universities but studying the same subject is welcomed. There is a preference to be taught by people from business rather than academia, although it is recognised that some of these tutors may lack the teaching skills of a professional pedagogue. This can be manifest in trying to cover too much material within too short a period, failing to start at a basic enough level or going into too much technical detail.

> **❝The budding entrepreneur needs to know what is and is not patentable, the benefits and drawbacks of patenting, and have a general idea of the process and costs involved. ❞**

For example, the budding entrepreneur needs to know what is and is not patentable, the benefits and drawbacks of patenting, and have a general idea of the process and costs involved. A patent agent may be tempted, however, to spend a lot of time on the minutiae of the filing process along with timing deadlines and so on, resulting in the student being overwhelmed with information and failing to grasp the most significant points that have to be considered in any business strategy.

Students generally prefer to be taught in a systematic manner, building from one concept to another rather than taking individual stand-alone courses, and would prefer to spread the course over a more conventional academic term or year rather than attend intensive workshops in the form of, say, a summer school which inevitably must pack in so much information that many students either find it difficult to keep up or are unable to absorb all the information that is put before them. Spreading classes over time also permits students to more effectively consider the information provided in the context of their own area of study or business interest.

For those universities with access to a pool of appropriate tutors scheduling such a programme within the normal academic year, and where timetabling can be flexible, would not be particularly difficult, but others who are dependent on bringing in tutors from some distance away may not have this luxury and may still have to look at providing more intensive opportunities. Perhaps in these situations some thought might be given to using distance learning techniques and webcasts to support the more intense face-to-face sessions.

A number of universities are now looking to integrate courses of this nature into their postgraduate offerings, however there is a cost involved and it may be that this sort of training cannot be offered initially across-the-board. One option may be to offer these courses in those departments where students most frequently end up self-employed, such as journalism or law, or departments from which spin-outs are most common, which depending on the university might be some branches of engineering or informatics. Skills which are most relevant for establishing a business will of course also be significant for those joining small companies and this may be another area that universities should consider.

A less costly approach that might be taken with students who have already formulated ideas for a business would be to establish *alternative boards* or *mastermind groups* whereby a group of student entrepreneurs supported by a facilitator would get together on a regular basis to discuss a particular topic, say fundraising or marketing, in relation to their own businesses and to provide mutual support to each other. This form of self-mentoring is increasingly popular among established businesses and has the extra benefit of providing emotional support as well as practical skills. Additionally, it can effectively be used where the participants are establishing very different businesses and so may be a practical option for smaller universities that do not have the volume of start-ups to provide specific meetings for individual faculties.

Whatever option is taken there is clearly an interest amongst certain parts of the student body in obtaining this type of education and opportunities for the TTO to be involved in facilitating its provision, either directly or through the identification of potential subjects for study or tutors to deliver the material.

Conclusion

TTOs are here to stay and are offering an increasingly broad and professional service to academics and students. Resources are limited and so TTOs must be selective in the projects that they champion – to some extent this will be guided by the overall priorities of the university, whether that be to maximise educational opportunities for their student body, to support job creation within the immediate area, to hothouse high-prestige projects, or to maximise access to the university's research. Each group will have their own specific goals which will be reflected in the particular twists they give to their service offerings.

In this short article I have set out three areas where I believe TTOs could add value regardless of their overriding priorities. The development of a clear, transparent and fair complaints procedure could be carried out with minimal resources, as could the clarification of policy for the less conventional technology transfer project. In both cases use could probably be made of existing resources and processes and the result would be a considerable saving in time and money over the relatively short term.

A broad review of the educational opportunities in entrepreneurship within the university would clearly take more time and resources, and any implementation is likely also to involve individual departments and their particular interests and priorities. Many programmes do already exist within institutions though and it may be that elements of these could be fairly readily duplicated in other departments or made available in different formats to meet the specific needs of other groups. Where distances can be accommodated there may be merit in looking at sharing the supply of these programmes between similar departments in neighbouring institutions which would not only reduce costs but would encourage networking and provide students with alternative perspectives. Given the regular interaction of TTOs with industry and ongoing interest in the spin-outs of the university they are in a particularly good place to offer support in the establishment of these programmes.

8. Waking a Sleeping Giant: Commercialising University Research

By Roya Ghafele

Knowledge transfer – not technology transfer

Economic history illustrates that a lack of adequate leverage and transfer of any type of knowledge, be it explicit, tacit or organisational knowledge, leads to stagnation. In Europe, growth rates remained constant for nearly 1500 years after the fall of the Roman Empire for partly this reason; 'the 18th century elites of Great Britain earned about the same as the elites of Rome in the 3rd century AD'.[1]

It was only during the industrial revolution that economic growth began again, at a drastic rate. The practical application of various knowledge systems and inventions in business, transport and machinery that became possible during the industrial revolution meant that economic processes could be optimised and both producer and consumer surplus be achieved. These important macroeconomic shifts were strongly driven by adequate knowledge transfer processes between academics and inventors on the one side and business on the other side. This is an important lesson from history as it illustrates the crucial role that knowledge transfer plays in economic performance and underlines the dire need to ensure the adequate transfer of knowledge from universities to business as well as from business to universities.

While the detailed mechanisms of the interplay of knowledge creation and economic growth have been discussed in great detail by endogenous growth theory, this paper is interested in assessing the role that universities play in the knowledge-based economy.[2] It does so using the example of best practice scenarios, as currently being undertaken by the University of Oxford, the University of California, Berkeley, the Massachusetts Institute of Technology (MIT) and Chalmers University of Technology. It argues that key to successful research commercialisation is the leverage of clusters that assure knowledge flows between universities and business.

Despite the lack of a consensual definition, two features of clusters are widely recognised: agglomeration, 'the geographical concentration of a specific industry and related activities'; and inter-connection, where the mix of competitive-cooperative relationships between local actors generates better performance in terms of employment, productivity and knowledge transfer.[3] Cooperation among local actors minimises costs and increases the value extracted, fosters spillovers, increasing the efficiency of various enterprises, and enables the sharing of infrastructure, knowledge and marketing. Many definitions of clusters highlight the routine interaction of institutional policies and economic actors.[4] Cluster analysis thus coincides with recent approaches highlighting the role of law in structuring economic exchange as it accentuates the systematic relationship that exists between economic life and legal institutions.[5]

I call this the *third way* of university research commercialisation, which focuses on systemic change rather than on single stakeholder intervention. It reflects a novel generation of knowledge policies that focuses on training, awareness raising and the leverage of cluster effects, rather than the development of physical infrastructure (such as science parks).

The third way of research commercialisation

The third way of research commercialisation is a unique approach that outperforms existing best practice in many ways; it focuses on the leverage of networks among the various academic institutions, rather than repeating the traditional *one university – one technology transfer office* approach. The *third way* also outperforms existing best practices by adopting latest trends in

❝The *third way* of research commercialisation focuses on the leverage of networks among the various academic institutions.❞

intellectual property management, such as trading IP on online platforms like those provided by the Intellectual Property Exchange International (IPXI), perceiving intellectual property as a financial asset and leveraging open innovation for improving patent quality. Organisational values, structures and procedures of various actors (business, academia, government) are recognised and different institutional cultures are sought to be overcome through boundary spanning. The competing demands and interests of business and academia are reflected through the introduction of socially responsible university research commercialisation, as currently undertaken at the University of California at Berkeley.

The third way stands in strong contrast to an early generation of technology transfer efforts, which primarily sought to assure spillover effects from universities to business through the creation of science parks and the provision of other physical infrastructure. The very term *technology transfer* implicitly

❝The competing demands and interests of business and academia are reflected through the introduction of socially responsible university research commercialisation.❞

includes some outdated features as it incites that commercially valuable knowledge is primarily found in the hard sciences (natural sciences) and its transfer is best assured through the provision of expensive physical infrastructure. The social sciences and humanities are thereby cut out from any technology transfer efforts. This rudimentary view of knowledge generation and exchange not only reflects an inadequate approach towards knowledge management, but also a one-sided view on universities.

I argue that the third way of research commercialisation reflects best the essence of knowledge. Knowledge is an intangible good. Its worth does not decrease the more it is in use. On the contrary; the more it is being used, the more it becomes valuable. Thus, knowledge delivers increasing returns as it is more widely adopted. The more it is adopted, the more experience is gained and the more it is improved.

Knowledge generation is associated with non-predictability and potential inefficiencies. It is a complex process that is undergone to solve complex problems and the component-based nature of knowledge's production means that the modular division of labour can be easily aggregated into a final structure. This modular division makes individual contributions highly effective and beneficial to a given project. The cost of collaboration in these various endeavours decreases, the more exchange takes place. That is why it is so important to emphasise networks and the establishment of functioning clusters. The management of intangible capital functions best through the establishment of a functioning intangible infrastructure. This requires commonly established notions of what a university is to be slightly altered.

The role of universities in the knowledge economy

The economic contribution of universities has for a long time been seen through the lens of training the next generation of the labour force. Universities have also been seen as contributing to new perspectives on established views. In some ways universities have come to be stylised as cultural artefacts that serve primarily the greater public good but they are much more than that. Say Ryan and Ghafele:

> 'Universities are much more than the depositories of various knowledge islands. They are neither dictionaries nor databases; they are the "know-how" and "know-why" institutions in any healthy knowledge economy. Universities dispose of the organisational capabilities to turn information and know-how into commercially valuable products and services. The collective knowledge, know-how, and learning maintained by the university, its so-called "core competency", is difficult for a competing business to replicate.'[6]

The knowledge that is embedded in universities and managed through deliberate knowledge transfer is the ultimate source of competitive advantage in the marketplace, whether of economy, polity, or society.[7]

Universities play an important role in the knowledge ecosystem. I use the term *ecosystem* because it reflects how the creation of knowledge is a process that involves multiple actors that interact in a complex manner. Innovation is the process of extracting value from ideas and creativity; it is frequently associated with discontinuous change and a process of creative destruction.[8] Innovation relates to both the transformation of an existing idea into a new product or the improvement of an existing product or operational process. It is a complex process where new ideas, objects and practices are created, developed or reinvented.[9] This process is related to the introduction and application of ideas within a specific role, group or organisation.[10] It is most commonly associated with new processes, products, procedures and outcomes. The adequate interplay between universities and companies is an important element that helps trigger these processes and underlines the importance of clusters.

It is important to underline that the primary function of universities is not 'to turn science into business,' but to advance the existing knowledge foundations of humanity.[11] In this sense it is important to optimise the interplay between universities and business if and where it is appropriate. In order to do so it is however important to understand that knowledge within universities experiences a different type of institutionalisation from knowledge that exists within business.

This paper is structured as follows: I first discuss the different institutional structures of universities and business, then explain the important role that intellectual property plays in mediating between the different institutional realities of business and academia. I then proceed to present a series of case studies that illustrate the argument. I conclude by offering five key recommendations that I deem essential for the successful transfer of knowledge from universities to business.

The business model of a university

Within the academic literature a business model has come to be seen as the creation of value and the implementation of strategy to capture revenue from this value. A successful business model relies on two key elements: *value creation* and *value appropriation*.[12] On the business model, Ghafele and Gibert say:

> 'The business model establishes the organisational, procedural and operational means by which a firm creates and appropriates value in its target market. Value creation involves all of the resources and processes deployed towards product strategy and logistical strategy. Value appropriation describes the revenue logic of the firm's operations.'[13]

This understanding is underlined by Henry Chesbrough's definition of a business model as the provision of some sort of value to third parties, from which the business derives profits, which is a result of the firm's cost structure and its turnover.[14] This definition is not fundamentally different from what constitutes a university, only that the type of value that may be offered to third parties is somewhat different. But, then again, businesses are characterised by heterogeneity in services and products they provide. Another similarity is that, like in companies, the knowledge generated within universities belongs to the university (following the Bayh-Dole Act and its European variations). I thus argue that from a mere academic point of view no clear distinction can be made between a firm and a university.

The main difference that does exist is political in nature. The access to education is in most countries considered a civil right and university education is either provided through the state or with the support of state subsidies. In economic terms, this is the public provision of a private good. This artificial intervention of the regulator is probably the most important feature that distinguishes a university from a company. The public or semi-public structure of most universities triggers substantially different incentive structures for universities and business.

> **"From a mere academic point of view no clear distinction can be made between a firm and a university."**

This is important as essentially any business that were turned into a public or semi-public institution would experience the same type of shift in incentive structures. While it is beyond the scope of this piece to discuss in greater depth the economic rationale of public or semi-public institutions, I do need to elaborate the different organisational mechanisms of knowledge generation and transfer in various settings. This is important because identifying these differences helps us to understand the challenges of knowledge transfer from universities to business and provides a baseline for improving the present situation.

The entire academic system is based on knowledge sharing and putting knowledge subsequently into the public domain. In fact, academic success is measured by how much knowledge academics succeed in putting into the public domain, be it through journal articles or through lectures and talks in public. The more an academic is quoted by peers, the better their career prospects. The academic model of knowledge generation and knowledge sharing is thus in many ways similar to the *open source* movement. Like in open source, many different scientists contribute to the deliberate reflection on a scientific problem and it is the joint effort that may lead to a possible solution. Similar to open source, academics have an incentive to put their knowledge in the public domain as they gain an indirect benefit from doing so. Putting knowledge in the public domain increases the academic's reputational capital, which in turn may lead to better career prospects.

There are therefore striking similarities between the motivations for academics to share knowledge and the motivations of open source programmers. While knowledge is being put in the public domain, revenues can be generated through the provision of complementary services. In the case of open source, this may be a range of supplementary services that are offered in addition

> ❝ **Academic success is measured by how much knowledge academics succeed in putting into the public domain, be it through journal articles or through lectures and talks in public.** ❞

to the free software. In the case of academia, the knowledge that is given away for free helps the academic in return to apply for research funding, scholarships and better paid teaching positions. Owning various forms of intellectual property, such as patents, has so far hardly been considered a prestigious asset and leads to far less reputational capital than an extensive publication track record.

Also, the IP generated by academics belongs in most countries to the university and not the individual researcher, which brings along a classical *principal-agent* situation, where the interests of the agent (the academic) and the principal (the university) are not aligned and the agent will seek to act her own personal benefits, which do not necessarily coincide with those of the principal. The academic model of knowledge generation is thus fundamentally different from the intellectual property system and the ownership of patents or other forms of IP is in most instances seen as an additional burden, rather than a winning opportunity.

> ❝ **There are striking similarities between the motivations for academics to share knowledge and the motivations of open source programmers.** ❞

Many academics also simply don't know what intellectual property is and how they could use IP ownership for their own advantage. It seems that most technology transfer offices of universities tend to not fully realise that they encounter a century-old tradition of knowledge management that is fundamentally at odds with the intellectual property system.

While the *open source* business model of academic research has succeeded in advancing our understanding of the most varied phenomena, it does not lend itself necessarily as the best means to structure the interaction between universities and companies. As universities leave knowledge in the public domain, companies are free to pick and choose from existing stocks of knowledge as they please. As academics took the deliberate choice to put knowledge in the public domain, they have also given up the right to ownership of this knowledge. This means they have no say over what is to happen with this knowledge and under what conditions firms may use the university's knowledge capital. It also bears the risk that market participants are deprived of the incentive to take the knowledge further and bring it to the market in the form of commercially viable products and services.

From a societal point of view the mere reliance on indirect benefits from publicly available knowledge means that knowledge is insufficiently transferred and that costs associated with knowledge generation increase, which in turn may lead to slowing economic growth.[15] These increased costs of knowledge generation result in part from inadequate leverage of existing knowledge assets and the corresponding duplication of effort among various actors. Assuring the adequate protection of university knowledge through intellectual property is ultimately a matter of degree. Protecting knowledge through intellectual property is associated with costs, which in turn may mean that research becomes more expensive and academics may focus on easily attainable research outputs so as to remain competitive in the search for research funding.[16]

" There is a need to establish collaborative structures that enable a functioning value chain from knowledge generation to final product/service. "

It is not the primary purpose of the university to generate commercially relevant knowledge, but to provide novel perspectives on established views. Academia does not exist to make a profit, but to generate knowledge, nor does it dispose of the mechanisms to commercialise knowledge as widely and broadly as possible. But business does. Thus, there is a need to establish collaborative structures that enable a functioning value chain from knowledge generation to final product/service.

Knowledge transfer as social interaction

Knowledge transfer may be seen as a 'process through which ideas and techniques generated at one place find their application at another place. Thanks to this process innovation reaches out to members of a social system through various means of communication'.[17] Thus knowledge transfer may be seen as a process and a continuous interaction.[18]

As the transfer of knowledge is essentially a social interaction, it is important to ensure that this social interaction functions as smoothly as possible. The transfer of knowledge contains various processes that foster the flow of know-how, experiences, knowledge and tools, and aims at offering an optimised and cheaper solution.[19] The transfer of knowledge can however be expensive – for example opportunity costs such as the shift from fundamental research to applied research can be substantial – and it may not necessarily lead to desired results.

If we perceive knowledge transfer as a social process, then it becomes evident why it is important to understand in the first instance the different incentive structures of the various players. Any type of successful knowledge transfer needs to ensure that the partners involved in the knowledge transfer process have a motivation to be so and that they find themselves in a situation that allows them to exchange their knowledge freely and without constraint.

The chart below seeks to illustrate the various elements that are needed in a virtuous knowledge transfer system.[20] In order to provide adequate incentives for academics and students, faculty and student involvement in the knowledge commercialisation process must be rewarded. It needs to be considered in the annual performance review of academics and it should help students find jobs once they graduate. Furthermore, boundary spanning needs to be promoted. The existing cultural and informational barriers among business and academia need to be overcome through the provision of adequate forums of exchange and information channels. Networking opportunities need to be provided to guarantee an informal exchange and natural knowledge spillover effects.

This is why the creation of adequate social linkages and clusters is more important than the provision of physical infrastructure.

Knowledge transfer can take various forms. In most of these forms intellectual property plays an important role and acts as a channel for the transfer of knowledge. Yet, many academics do not know a lot about intellectual property and its economic relevance. That is why there is a need for IP entrepreneurship and awareness raising programmes. The adequate institutional support needs to be assured through decentralised brokerage. Rather than have one single technology transfer office that acts like a monopoly, better results can be achieved by decentralising technology transfer and making everyone in the university feel that technology transfer is their cause. This approach reflects an open innovation approach, where every stakeholder in the university is involved, rather than just a few people working in the technology transfer office.

ff Rather than have one single technology transfer office that acts like a monopoly, better results can be achieved by decentralising technology transfer and making everyone in the university feel that technology transfer is their cause. 🥚🥚

While knowledge transfer can be embedded in research collaborations, contractual research or the licensing of research output, transaction costs associated with the transfer of knowledge can be controlled by using IP online exchanges, fostering IP brokerage and IP fairs. The university may also consider attracting investors who help promote the virtuous cycle of university knowledge transfer by providing the necessary funding and can in exchange have an option on future returns.

Developing a knowledge transfer system: creating leverage for cooperation and clusters

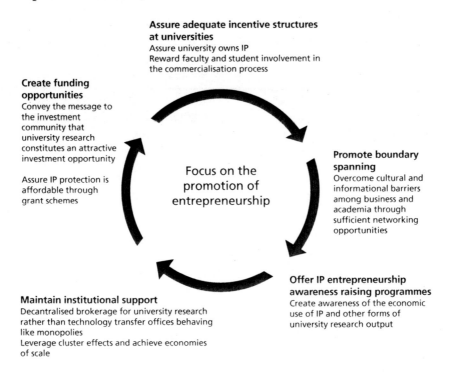

Assure adequate incentive structures at universities
Assure university owns IP
Reward faculty and student involvement in the commercialisation process

Create funding opportunities
Convey the message to the investment community that university research constitutes an attractive investment opportunity

Assure IP protection is affordable through grant schemes

Focus on the promotion of entrepreneurship

Promote boundary spanning
Overcome cultural and informational barriers among business and academia through sufficient networking opportunities

Offer IP entrepreneurship awareness raising programmes
Create awareness of the economic use of IP and other forms of university research output

Maintain institutional support
Decantralised brokerage for university research rather than technology transfer offices behaving like monopolies
Leverage cluster effects and achieve economies of scale

Source: Roya Ghafele

The mediating function of intellectual property rights

'Intangible assets can be the source of competitive advantage only if they are supported by a regime of strong appropriability or are non-tradeable or sticky.'[21]

The introduction of intellectual property rights establishes property rights over knowledge. This is in my view the most important economic function of IP. The privatisation of clearly codified knowledge that has been made fully explicit constitutes an important element for the establishment of a market-based economy. De Soto, for example, observes that developing countries remain poor in spite of a wealth of natural resources because of a lack of respect for property rights. The inadequate guarantee of private property prevents the development of prospering markets.[22]

A parallel may be drawn here to *intellectual* property. The existing judicial system gives way to the creation of markets for knowledge and the transfer of knowledge in a clear and transparent form. In this way, intellectual property may be seen as the currency of the knowledge-based economy. The architecture provided through IP allows the leverage not only of the *use value* of intellectual property, but also its *exchange value*.[23] This means that knowledge may serve various purposes and that the existence of IP may give lead to secondary markets for knowledge, decoupled from primary knowledge markets.

The introduction of private property over knowledge allows the creation of surplus value. To offer a simplistic comparison, one is able to extract value from land even without owning it. One can go, for example, into the woods and collect fruits. However if one owns land, then one can create value that may be decoupled from the land's primary function. One can start trading the land and that trade may have really nothing to do any more with the primary function of the land. Precisely these mechanisms are made possible through IP and for this very reason the existence of IP plays an important role in knowledge transfer. It gives way to a new paradigm of what constitutes property rights.

Like other forms of property rights, intellectual property rights are artefacts. To what extent knowledge should be turned into a private property is ultimately a political decision. Access conditions remain an important element that does need careful deliberation and policy action. It is important to ensure that the public interest is being maintained and that, besides commercial considerations, the freedom of research is assured. This is even more important as knowledge transfer between universities and business constitutes a transfer between (semi) public and private institutions.

If intellectual property is being perceived as an option that gives way to economic interaction, then it becomes obvious that intellectual property rights allow the owner to create value. Buying, selling, trading, licensing or donating IP for free becomes possible through the establishment of property rights over knowledge. Intellectual property makes knowledge explicit and in this sense separates the knowledge creator from the knowledge. The dilemma associated with tacit knowledge is overcome.

IP also makes it possible to hedge against various risks associated with the creation of new knowledge. Knowledge generation can sometimes be a search for the metaphorical needle in the hay. While IP cannot minimise the risk associated with the search for new knowledge, it provides a compensation scheme for the research efforts that were associated with this search. This being said, Scherer and Harhoff document that only 10% of an average patent portfolio disposes of commercially relevant value.[24]

❝ As most universities watch their patents very closely but tend to ignore other forms of academic proprietary expressions, academics remain by and large unconstrained to use these other forms of IP as they see fit. ❞

Finally, it is misleading to associate intellectual property primarily with patents. Intellectual property comprises the most various forms of creative expression. Copyrights and related rights, trademarks, trade secrets, design rights and protection against unfair competition all allow academics across all disciplines to protect their intellectual property. Yet, there is an overarching lack of awareness of other forms of intellectual property. Paradoxically, this has helped mitigate the *principal-agent* dilemma that universities face in their knowledge management. As most universities watch their patents very closely but tend to ignore other forms of academic proprietary expressions, academics remain by and large unconstrained to use these other forms of IP as they see fit.

Case studies

In order to assess the practical implications of the arguments made above, I have chosen some case studies. I have selected MIT, the University of California at Berkeley, the University of Oxford and Chalmers University of Technology in Sweden. I chose these cases as they reflect in our view current best practice in university knowledge transfer. Also, the author is personally familiar with Berkeley and Oxford, having worked in both institutions.

Chalmers University is interesting as it is not very famous and operates in a country with high taxes that is strongly oriented towards social welfare goals. Thus the institutional context in which Chalmers finds itself is completely different from that of the US and the UK universities. Yet, the way Chalmers commercialises its knowledge replicates very much the decentralised knowledge transfer system I propose.

Berkeley is interesting as it is one of the few schools that assures that knowledge transfer is undertaken in a socially responsible way. Successful knowledge transfer is not only expressed in monetary terms, but also through the provision of public welfare. With respect to IP, Berkeley promotes open innovation clauses and issues non-exclusive licensing arrangements on a broad scale.

I assessed the case study sample according to common features and applied strategies in research funding. The analysis was based on publicly available secondary information and no interviews were conducted with staff members. I believe that a further in-depth examination of these case studies could be a valuable area for future research. The significant gaps that exist between US universities and European universities may be explained by a different political economy in which European and US universities find themselves. Thus, there is a certain lack of comparability of data. When studying these four cases, I was interested in trying to understand where major sources of funding come from; what knowledge commercialisation strategies were employed; and what initiatives had been launched to realise superior value from knowledge.

Sources of funding

MIT, Berkeley, Oxford and Chalmers focus on research funding from: business and NGOs; funding for spin offs and revenues from consulting; and royalties and licences

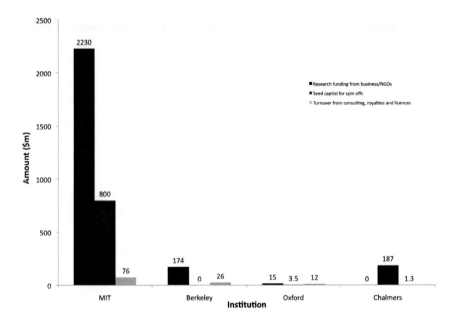

Source: Roya Ghafele, websites of institutions.

Oxford: Revenues from consulting not fully monitored; Chalmers: Research funding from business/NGOs not monitored; Berkeley: Seed capital for spin offs not monitored

When looking at the major sources of funding, one common feature emerges. All universities generate funding from the same type of sources; namely research funding from business and NGOs, seed capital for spin-outs and income from consulting, royalties, and licences from intellectual property. Certainly, MIT is unrivalled in its overarching income streams, but this can be explained by the different institutional context the MIT operates within, the strong reputation the school has, as well as the solid alumni network of the university.

Chalmers university again attracts a lot of seed capital for its spin-outs, which reflects the entrepreneurial spirit of the school and the strong orientation towards knowledge entrepreneurship in most areas that the school is providing training in. From a structural point of view this analysis suggests that successful knowledge transfer is multifaceted and needs to reflect a solid mix of revenues from IP, consulting, venture capital (VC), funding from angels, and other institutional funding for spin-outs, and research funding from the wider community. This is illustrated in the chart above.[25]

Knowledge commercialisation strategies

All case study universities leverage many channels to commercialise university research

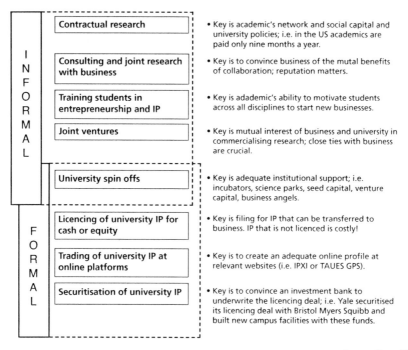

Source: Roya Ghafele

All universities I studied leverage a variety of channels to commercialise their knowledge. Both formal and informal channels are used to reach out to the widest audience. Channels of commercialisation can range from contractual research, to consulting and joint ventures with business, to training students in entrepreneurship and particularly in intellectual property. Among the more formal channels of university research commercialisation are the licensing of university research in exchange for cash or equity, the trading of IP at online platforms, such as the Chicago based Intellectual Property Exchange International, or the securitisation of intellectual property. The various channels require different skill sets and different approaches to ensure that mutual interests are aligned.

In order to promote consulting and other informal means of knowledge exchange it is important that university policy enables such an exchange. In many universities in continental Europe, academics are not even allowed to consult for business. On the other extreme are US universities which only pay a salary for nine months in a year and expect academics to earn an income from another source during the other three months of the year. The University of Oxford is somewhat between these two positions as it allows academics to consult for 30 days in any given calendar year.

Formal means of exchange require adequate institutional support. Incubators, good contacts with venture capital firms and business angels are crucial for spinning out companies from universities. Other formal channels, such as the online trading or securitisation of IP, are quite new and have mainly been used in US contexts. These certainly constitute arising opportunities for universities. All of this is summarised in the chart above.[26]

Realising value from knowledge

University research commercialisation initiatives

Initiative	MIT	Berkeley	Oxford	Chalmers
University owns IP	■	■	■	
IP awareness training on campus				■
Government grants/public support for IP protection	■	■	■	■
Socially responsible IP transfer and open source		■		
Entrepreneurship education	■	■	■	■
Business plan development programmes	■	■		■
Advisory services, external consulting firms	■	■	■	■
Student entrepreneurship organisations	■	■		■
Commercialisation services on campus	■	■		■
External service provider for commercialisation	■	■	■	■
University on-campus incubator	■	■		■
Outside incubators situated in town	■	■		■
Seed capital	■	■		■
University shares in spin offs and licences	■	■		■
Official incentives for commercialisation				■

Source: Roya Ghafele, Rasmusen et al., *Technovation* 26 (2006) 518-533, websites of institutions

Structural similarities can also be observed when looking at the various initiatives universities take to the commercialisation of research. All universities have spin-out and licence programmes, incubators, external service providers situated within proximity of the university, and commercialisation services on campus. All are surrounded by consulting firms – such as Oxfirst Limited or Oxford Analytica in Oxford – that seek to transfer university knowledge to business.

Emphasis on public support for IP protection and government grants is also assured in the universities I studied. At Chalmers the individual researcher and not the university owns the IP. This may be the reason why knowledge transfer in Sweden is so decentralised. Official incentives for university research commercialisation exist also only in Sweden, where the government has established specialised commercialisation agencies in major university regions. Chalmers is also the only university to offer extensive training on intellectual property across various faculties. Thus, it is not only taught in the law school. This is important in that it recognises the practical influence of intellectual property on all academic fields and encourages awareness of intellectual property beyond a purely legal perspective. This is summarised in the chart above.[27]

Conclusion

Knowledge transfer between university and business is conventionally justified by the university's ability to train the next generation of labour force and to ensure spillover from the engineering and natural sciences departments, which has genuinely been viewed to be best achieved through the development of physical infrastructure. The rationale I propose for the transfer of knowledge is entirely different: knowledge transfer is understood as a social process that is best achieved through the provision of an adequate intangible infrastructure. This infrastructure comprises the development of networks, clusters and adequate incentive structures within the universities.

Knowledge is intangible in nature and it can best be transferred through a systemic approach that adequately grasps its intangible nature. Within that context it is important to understand IP as an enabling mechanism. IP can be an instrument that empowers universities because it increases the economic advantages derived from research and precipitates a governance structure owned and operated by the university. The potential benefits of this governance structure are supported by cluster research emphasising social cohesion, good management, trust and collaboration, community culture, ethics and university leadership.[28]

Successful knowledge transfer is neither black nor white; it is a matter of degree. This paper sought to sketch out knowledge transfer as a social process that is driven by economic actors with various incentive structures. It has been argued that knowledge transfer is not primarily driven by the provision of physical infrastructure, but the adequate provision of an intangible infrastructure that enables economic actors to come together, exchange knowledge in an informal way and trade it for their mutually beneficial interest. In order to make this happen, it is important that the university's policies reward such activities, which is an important element to change the widely established custom of putting knowledge only in the public domain. Recommendations for how this can be done are given at the end of this chapter.

> **❝ Knowledge transfer is understood as a social process that is best achieved through the provision of an adequate intangible infrastructure. This infrastructure comprises the development of networks, clusters and adequate incentive structures within the universities. ❞**

The cases I presented are at the forefront of university knowledge commercialisation and may serve as best practice examples for a range of continental European universities. Many of them still lag behind in adopting initiatives that enable and promote boundary spanning between universities and business. This article sought to explain using the example of practical cases what successful university research transfer can look like and what elements need to be considered. The universities I studied generate funding from three major areas: research funding from business and NGO; spin-outs; and revenues from intellectual property and consulting assignments.

Successful research financing is multifaceted

Description of policy framework

Incentive structures
• Vest IP ownership within the university
• Develop socially responsible research transfer
• Recognise engagement with business as part of
  academic achievement

Boundary spanning
• Leverage online platforms and social networks
• Expand existing MOUs and assure knowledge transfers
• Focus on involving students in the commercialisation
  process

IP entrepreneurship awareness
• Develop training material on IP entrepreneurship
• Undertake awareness raising seminars
• Supply outreach material to multipliers

Institutional support
• Promote incubators
• Create research commercialisation scouts
• Sponsor university-wide research transfer institution(s)
• Increase patent quality through peer to patent

Adequate funding
• Make IP filing affordable
• Revise financial reporting standards for intangibles
• Standardise IP valuation procedures
• Assure royalties are not subject to taxation

Designed to achieve

Research funding from business/NGOs

Funding for spin offs and spin off
creation

Revenues from royalties, licences and
consulting

Entrepreneurship

Source: Roya Ghafele

In the chart above I have summarised the five areas that are most needed to continuously grow revenues from existing income channels. In order to provide adequate incentive structures it is important to recognise engagement with business as part of the academic achievement. To assure boundary spanning the necessary social platforms need to be maintained and further developed. Online platforms, such as LinkedIn, can be very helpful to maintain relations with potential partners. University alumni networks form an equally important channel that helps commercialise university research.

Lack of awareness of both intellectual property and entrepreneurship can be overcome through training and awareness-raising programmes. Rather than have centralised courses, decentralised training through awareness raising scouts may be preferable. Further institutional support may be promoted through decentralised university research transfer institutions and by assuring that intellectual property protection remains affordable. All of this is summarised in the chart above.

Recommendations[29]

Based on this analysis I recommend the following steps for successful knowledge transfer:

Provide incentive structures for knowledge transfer

- Assure that the performance review of faculty members includes off-campus activities in addition to research and teaching

- Reward faculty members for conducting research in partnership with non-academic-professionals

- Assure faculty members have the freedom to choose if they want to engage in applied research and business projects

- Assure that university policies allow the knowledge transfer and that academics do not act outside the law when collaborating with business

- Develop socially responsible knowledge transfer strategies and ask academics to comply with these norms

Promote boundary spanning

- Develop performance plans that measure to what extent cooperation with organisations outside the university improves research activities

- Seek to develop at the departmental level relationships with private or public sector institutions, as well as seed capital

- Develop a reputation for collaborating with business and seek to be highly regarded by business/investors. Get recognised by business and society for flexibility and innovativeness

- Leverage online platforms and social networks

- Expand existing Memoranda of Understanding (MOUs) and ensure knowledge transfers

- Focus on involving students in the commercialisation process

Develop IP awareness raising programmes

- Teach entrepreneurial skill sets and business aspects of IP across the university

- Assure faculty members are aware of IP and recognise the potential commercial applicability of research

- Assure that the university is very responsive to new ideas and innovative practices

- Help students to secure high-quality industry positions

- Develop training material on IP entrepreneurship

- Undertake awareness-raising seminars

- Supply outreach material to multipliers

Guarantee a high level of institutional support

- Develop university-wide departments/groups/individuals dedicated to business/university liaison activities

- Seek to benefit from the proximity of science parks and incubators

- Use feedback to improve institutional support for commercial activity

- Create positions for research commercialisation scouts

- Foster university-wide research transfer institution(s)

Be creative in identifying new funding opportunities

- Seek significant funding from sources other than the government

- Generate off-campus benefits from research projects

- Generate income from university spin-outs, licensing out IP, consulting and contractual research

- Inspire students to use their education to scope new business opportunities and start new firms

- Make IP filing affordable and ensure royalties are not subject to taxation

This article advances earlier work I did for the Austrian Council for Research and Tecyhnology. R. Ghafele 2009; IPR und Technologie in Oesterreich. Eine Analyse aus der Perspektive der Neuen Institutionellen Oekonomie.

www.rat-fte.at/publikationenen.htm

Endnotes

[1] W. J. Baumol, *The Free Market Innovation Machine* (Princeton University Press, 2002), pp. 3, 14. Quoted in M. J. Ryan, 'IP and Economic Growth', Creative and Innovative Economy Center Discussion, note 1.

[2] See for example P. Romer, 'Increasing Returns and Long-Run Growth', *Journal of Political Economy* 94 (1986); P. Romer, 'Endogenous Technological Change', *Journal of Political Economy* 98 (1990).

[3] Santos, A. Almeida, and A. Teixeira, 'Searching for Clusters in Tourism. A Quantitative Methodological Proposal', FEP Working Papers 293, Universidade do Porto, Faculdade de Economia do Porto, 1-38 (2008).

[4] F. Capone, 'Regional Competitiveness in Tourist Local Systems', *44th European Congress of the European Regional Science Association (ERSA)*, 'Regions and Fiscal Federalism', University of Porto, Portugal (2004).

[5] N. Mercuro 'Toward a Comparative Institutional Approach to the study of Law and Economics', in N. Mercuro (ed) *Law and Economics*, Lancaster: Kluwer Academic Publishers, 1-27 (1989).

[6] M. Ryan and R. Ghafele, 'Do Patent Reforms Promote Innovation in Developing Countries? Evidence from Jordan and Brazil', George Washington University Discussion Paper (2007).

[7] H. L. Wilensky, *Organizational Intelligence: Knowledge and Policy in Government and Industry* (Basic Books, 1967); H. Demsetz, 'Toward a Theory of Property Rights', *American Economic Review* 5 (1972); K. Connor and C. K. Prahalad, 'Resource-Based Theory of the Firm: Knowledge Versus Opportunism', *Organization Science* 7 (1996).

[8] J. Schumpeter, *Capitalism, Socialism and Democracy* (Harper, 1942).

[9] M. Rogers, *The definition and measurement of innovation.* Melbourne Institute of Applied Economic and Social Research, (1998).

[10] J. L. King, V. Gurbaxani, K.L. Kraemer, F.W. McFarlan, KS Raman, and C.S. Yap, 'Institutional factors in information technology innovation', *Information Systems Research* 5 (2): 139-169 (1994).

[11] OECD Secretariat: Turning Science into Business: Patenting and Licensing at Public Research Organisations, OECD, Paris 2003. **www.oecd.org/document/2/0,2340,en_2649_34797_2513917_1_1_1_1,00.html**

[12] R. Rajala, M. Ross and V. Tuunainen, *Journal of Theoretical and Applied Electronic Commerce Research* Nr. 2/ 2 (2007).

[13] R. Ghafele, B. Gibert, 'Responsiveness Revolution', Credit Suisse Research Institute Report (2011).

[14] H. W. Chesbrough, 'Why Companies Should Have Open Business Models', *MIT Sloan Management Review*, 48:2 (2007).

[15] B. Hoekman, K. E. Maskus, K. Saggi, 'Transfer of Technology to Developing Countries: Unilateral and Multilateral Policy Options', World Bank Policy Research Working Paper 3332 (2004).

[16] C. Polster, 'How the Law Works: Exploring the Implications of Emerging Intellectual Property Regimes for Knowledge, Economy and Society', *Current Sociology* 49:4 (2001).

[17] J. Kirkland (ed.), *Barriers to International Technology Transfer* (Kluwer Academic Publishers, 1996).

[18] G. Bugliarello, N. Pak, A. Zhores, J. Moore (ed.), 'Technology Transfer. New Perspectives and Human Resources', Kluwer Law International. Dordrecht/Boston/London (1994); Centre de Développement de l'OCDE, Technologie et lutte contre la pauvreté en Asie et dans le Pacifique. OCDE Paris (2002); D. A. Dyker, *The Technology of Transition. Science and Technology Policies for Transition Countries* (Central University Press, Budapest, 1997); J-S, Shin, *The Economics of the Latecomers. Catching-up, technology transfer and institutions in Germany, Japan and South Korea* (Routledge, 1996); A. Boutat, *Les Transferts Internationaux de Technologie* (Presse Universitaire de Lyon, 1991); A. Boutat, *Relations Technologiques Internationales: Mécanismes et enjeux* (Presse Universitaire de Lyon, 1991).

[19] UNFCC, Advance Report on Recommendations on Future Financing Options for Enhancing the Development, Deployment, Diffusion, and Transfer of Technologies Under the Convention, the United Nations Framework Convention on Climate Change, Bonn, 1-10 June 2009, quoted from D. Sandor.

[20] R. Ghafele, 'Financing University Research', **ipfinance.blogspot.com/2011/03/waking-sleeping-giant.html**

[21] D. J. Teece, 'Profiting from Technological Innovation: Implications for Integration, Collaboration, Licensing, and Public Policy', *Research Policy* 15 (1987).

[22] H. de Soto, *The Mystery of Capital: Why Capitalism Triumphs in the West and Fails Everywhere Else* (Basic Books, 2000).

[23] N. Rudisill, 'Essay 1: Please assess the strengths, weaknesses, opportunities and threats [SWOT] of a system of proprietary knowledge as a means to organize innovation?' Class on Global Governance of Innovation by R. Ghafele (2010).

[24] F. M. Scherer, D. Harhoff, 'Technology policy for a world of skew-distributed outcomes', Research Policy, Nr. 29 (2000).

[25] R. Ghafele, 'Financing University Research', **ipfinance.blogspot.com/2011/03/waking-sleeping-giant.html**

[26] R. Ghafele, 'Financing University Research', **ipfinance.blogspot.com/2011/03/waking-sleeping-giant.html**

[27] E. Rasmussen, Ø. Moen and M. Gulbrandsen, 'Initiatives to promote commercialization of university knowledge', *Technovation*, Nr. 26: (2006).

[28] F. M. Santos, K. M. Eisenhardt, 'Constructing Markets and Shaping Boundaries: Entrepreneurial Power in Nascent Fields', *The Academy of Management Journal*, Nr. 52:4 (2009).

[29] R. Ghafele, 'Financing University Research', **ipfinance.blogspot.com/2011/03/waking-sleeping-giant.html**

9. Academic Research and Commercialisation

By Alexander Weedon

Background

Academic institutions have the primary aim of developing and disseminating knowledge through teaching and research: this is a positive obligation to ensure that the endeavour of intellectual creativity is communicated to the world for the benefit of society. The exact wording of this obligation is laid out in the constitutional documents of every higher education institution (HEI). The Higher Education Funding Council (HEFCE), the body that regulates HEIs, suggests the following wording:

> 'The object of the HEI is, for the public benefit: to advance education, learning and research; to advance education, knowledge, and learning by teaching and research; to advance education and learning through the conduct and support of teaching and research.'[1]

The main conduit for the dissemination of intellectual output is by peer review journal and this has become the standard by which HEIs have been judged. In the UK this yardstick is described by the Research Assessment Exercise (RAE)[2] – to be replaced by the Research Excellence Framework (REF), which will be completed in 2014.[3] Through REF, HEIs in the UK are being strongly encouraged to be more inventive in demonstrating (and generating) public benefit by broadening the scope of how their work is judged to include research *impact*. The definition of impact is broad:

> 'The focus is on socio-economic impacts of any type and in any realm, realised outside the academic community… and should relate unambiguously and decisively to one or other aspects of a university department's research.'[4]

One of the ways for universities to demonstrate impact is to commercialise the vast wealth of intellectual property (IP) that they produce, not just to generate income or create financial gain but because for many disciplines – especially (although not exclusively) technical disciplines – putting that intellectual output into a product and selling that product into the marketplace is the main way that university research can directly benefit society.

Technology transfer and societal gain

Recent years have seen much discussion about the role of technology transfer in academia and, in particular, the place that commercialisation of technology occupies in HEIs. To a significant number of academic researchers, the very thought of commercial interests being involved in their work is abhorrent in the extreme and can be seen to affect impartiality.

The debate

Experience shows that the researchers' main concerns fall into two categories: should HEIs be involved in technology transfer at all; and are HEIs best placed to commercialise research? We have seen the debate that raged when Cambridge University changed their university statutes concerning the ownership of inventions made by academic staff, a debate that still rumbles on today.[5] Put simply, from 1999, Cambridge University put in motion a series of changes to university statutes that asserted the university's ownership of intellectual property created by researchers during the course of their employment. Traditionally this was held to be one of the rights of academic staff, to own and control the intellectual property they generate, but the changes were introduced to facilitate the exploitation of intellectual property, as well as enable the university to better manage the complex liabilities that now attend academic research. More recently the Wellings Report and Manchester Manifesto have encouraged debate on the matter.[6] It is no surprise that there is lively debate on the issues, since the answer to both of the questions posed at the start of this paragraph is *yes and no.*

On the *yes* side, university research is often very early-stage, without clear industrial application, and unpalatable to

❝ Experience shows that the researchers' main concerns fall into two categories: should HEIs be involved in technology transfer at all; and are HEIs best placed to commercialise research? ❞

potential licensees or investors until a significant amount of proof of concept and even product development work has been completed. So if a researcher's big idea is to have any chance at all of making the marketplace, to have real impact, the HEI has to step in to facilitate the process. This was clearly envisaged by the government when it set up the Higher Education Innovation Fund (HEIF).[7] The other role of technology transfer is to ensure that proper due diligence is carried out; that there are no encumbrances on the intellectual property; and, that in making a deal, the university is getting value for money and not saddled with unacceptable liabilities.

On the *no* side, academics believe that they should have complete freedom to decide what happens to the intellectual property they create in the course of their travails and, where a researcher chooses so to do, they are best placed to commercialise their intellectual property. Underlying this position is the real fear that technology transfer activities will impose restrictions on future research, which would be unacceptable.

Managing risk

Managing risk is important. HEIs, even those with experienced and well-developed technology transfer organs, such as UCL Business (UCL), King's Business (King's College London), ISIS (University of Oxford), Imperial Innovations (Imperial College), UMIP (University of Manchester), Cambridge Enterprise (University of Cambridge), etc., are not always in a position to see a product to market on their own, which is why they seek to partner with, or spin-out, companies that can attract the talent or investment required to do this. As described in more detail below, before a route to market can be decided upon, the main job of the technology transfer office is ensure that the university is free to commercialise: academic research in the modern era is surrounded by a web of obligations and liabilities to charitable funding bodies, to providers of materials, to industrial collaborators. All of these things need to be taken into account. This takes time, many months of intense planning and negotiation. In the absence of the professional staff that undertake these tasks it is unlikely that a researcher in full time employment would be able to dedicate their time to such activities.

Finance

Finance is often a key issue in university technology transfer: who pays for the costs of IP protection, legal bills and development expenses? Clearly, cash should not be diverted from research funds to undertake this commercial risk. It is also unlikely that the inventors themselves will have the financial wherewithal (or appetite for risk) required to make such a venture successful and so the right model needs to be adopted. Most of the large, research-intensive universities commercialise IP through a wholly-owned or a partially-owned subsidiary which offers the best balance of minimising risk, operational costs, patent expenses and legal risk by striving to be self-funding and professional, while maximising the benefits by aiming for the optimum deal terms.

Apart from being self-funded, such organisations have the ability to source external funding, like the large translational awards. They can also apply HEIF proof of concept funds and identify the right partners to take a project forward. HEIF proof of concept funding and other similar funds have been instrumental in seeing concepts transfer from the laboratory to the market. Without such funds and the guidance of technology transfer professionals, these ideas or materials would remain in laboratories. Technology transfer is also vital in obtaining large translational grants which require a commercial plan for exploitation of the results. For example, UCL Business' activities have been vital in securing over £30 million in such translation funding in the last three years, all of which is applied to research in the HEI.

Economics of societal gain

The economics of innovation development mean that IP protection is often required to attract the investment necessary to get products on the market.

Publishing an invention confers a small benefit on society as a whole; very few members of the public have ready access to academic journals and even fewer have the know-how to make use of the information contained within them in a way that will have a real impact on their daily lives. If researchers and their universities really want to benefit society, they have a duty to participate in technology transfer, which is the only way to acquire the funding and expertise necessary to realise the potential of the IP. Innovation is a key driving force of the economy because it means that new products are entering the market, creating more competition and encouraging more innovation.[8]

It has long been established that it is an economic imperative to give protection to companies for their innovations in order to allow them to recoup the costs of R&D, especially when not all R&D eventually leads to marketable innovations. This is even more important when we take a look at the regulatory situation for new drugs and chemical products. The patent system is designed to be a trade off; the state grants a monopoly in exchange for total disclosure of the invention.

> **❝ If researchers and their universities really want to benefit society, they have a duty to participate in technology transfer, which is the only way to acquire the funding and expertise necessary to realise the potential of the IP. ❞**

The reason for this is because, from an economic standpoint, the most efficient way to feel the benefits of innovation is to make it broadly available to the public, but in those circumstances innovation will be slow. Even with organisations such as universities, which are set up specifically to innovate and disseminate, the innovation will not make it to market without IP protection because no one with the ability to commercialise such innovation will do so without IP protection, particularly in the bio-pharmaceutical and chemical sectors where the actual innovation is only the beginning of a long and risky path to market. The social value of new innovation is high[9] but this does not take into account the vast expenditure required to take some high-tech innovations to market.

Despite the economic theory, commercialisation of research need not mean that profit is the only driving force; HEIs are examining other ways to get ideas and products into the marketplace through social enterprises, which provide an alternative route to ideas that are not attractive to industry entities.[10] In a recent debate organised by the Institute for Brand and Innovation Law (IBIL), Sir John Sulston, a signatory of the Manchester Manifesto, argued that academic freedom should be paramount and entirely free from commercial concerns and restrictions, but the system of capitalism that we work within is the reality we have to live with.[11]

Commercialisation of HEI IP goes beyond the immediate impact of job creation or cash generation – at its heart lies the principle of getting products that genuinely help people on to the market. Many HEIs are investing in this model, and some are experimenting with free access to IP.[12] Furthermore, this activity should not have any effect on researchers' freedoms or obligations inherent in their unique role. More importantly, inventors need to be intimately involved in the development and marketing of their ideas, to achieve the right balance of risk, reward, academic freedom and societal benefit.

Conflicting terms, conflicting interests

Academic research is now subject to a complex nexus of obligations; confidence, grant terms, material transfer agreements, research contracts, etc. Such obligations might go beyond IP considerations alone. These obligations are an increasingly unavoidable part of the academic environment and they should be taken seriously. Gone are the days when researchers could freely send or receive materials (even with their colleagues in the next lab), undertake collaborative research or accept grant funding without considering the legal ramifications of such activities. However, these legal barriers are not insurmountable and with proper management of legal terms they can be overcome if researchers think about possible restrictions and involve the HEI's professional support staff at an early stage.

Technology transfer office interactions with academic researchers demonstrate that in general they have a poor understanding of both the nature of contractual terms and IP rights. The basic issue seems to stem from a profound misunderstanding of the overriding importance of academic freedom over contractual or legal considerations and a profound short-termism born of the need to raise funding for research. Academic freedom, like all freedoms, is limited by the rules and regulations imposed upon it by the law and cannot be treated as a *get-out-of-jail-free card*.[13] HEIs are making concerted efforts to improve awareness of these issues to staff, including members of the HEI executive, who are also academic staff often with ongoing research duties of their own, but the prevailing attitude among academics is that such obligations can be ignored in the light of academic freedom. This means that grants administrators, technology transfer offices and research contracts staff are required to be extremely careful when conducting due diligence when they facilitate such interaction to ensure that there are no conflicting encumbrances, actual or potential, that could unreasonably limit academic freedom or leave the university in breach of any contractual terms.

From a commercialisation perspective this means ascertaining all of the interests that might exist in any academically-generated IP. This is probably one of the most time-consuming aspects of commercialisation and a key source of risk for our activities: identifying chains of title of arising IP can be very tricky where multiple organisations are involved. Thus a certain amount of pragmatism is required on the part of the support staff and the researchers to ensure that the benefits and risks of any proposed interaction with industry are properly weighed. HEIs need industry partners to help fund research to take technologies to market and the rewards can be good, both in terms of financial return and access to know-how or facilities, but in exchange those commercial partners expect a certain level of commercial rigour. This is also reflected in the terms for higher value translational awards that are available from charities such as the Wellcome Trust.[14]

Academic freedom is not a legally enforceable right that can be used as a defence for breach of contract or confidence per se. This means that, in order to preserve their academic freedom, academics need to be actively aware of the obligations that different funding imposes on their work and be careful about what terms they accept and how the terms might affect their ability to continue to work in their chosen field. They must also be prepared to walk away from deals that have these restrictions and heed the advice given by the professional staff. That is easier said than done as there is severe pressure on academic staff to fund their own work, particularly in the field of scientific research which is hugely expensive, a pressure that becomes more intense as academics become more senior, and a pressure that is not found in many other salaried roles. This causes researchers to agree to conflicting research terms (even against the advice of contracts staff) in order to get as much funding as they can without understanding the effect this has on their future research or the bigger picture for the HEI as a whole.

A common problem arises with material transfer agreements or collaboration contracts from industry partners that require ownership of arising IP to be transferred to them. Such terms preclude a lot of subsequent applications to charitable grants, whose terms require that arising IP is unencumbered. In addition, where queries are raised by contracts staff, the actions of the researcher can be backed up by deans and senior academics that have executive power, albeit with little or no understanding of the long-term legal ramifications of their decisions.

Research contracts and material transfer agreements with commercial entities are a common source of conflict and difficulty for HEIs. Research contracts cover research conducted at the university by a named researcher or group with specific expertise and will usually result in the creation of new and valuable IP. This is not to be confused with contract research undertaken by contract research organisations (CROs) – the difference is the individual or individuals involved. HEIs, especially those in high-rent areas such as UCL, are not able to compete with CROs for economic efficiency so the only reason industry will engage universities in a research contract is to gain access to the know-how and expertise that can be found there. This can provide valuable additional funding to researchers but these arrangements may place obligations on the researcher and HEI in relation to the IP arising from the work and any subsequent publications.

The Lambert Review

Following Richard Lambert's Review on Business-University Collaborations, a series of standardised agreements were developed to make it easier for industry and HEIs to collaborate based on five models.[15] These are shown in Table 9.1.

Table 9.1 – summary of Lambert model research agreements[16]

Model	Summary of terms	Arising IP resides
1	Sponsor has non-exclusive, non-sub-licensable rights to use in specified field/territory	HEI
2	Sponsor may negotiate further licence to some or all university IP	HEI
3	Sponsor may negotiate for an assignment of some university IP	HEI
4	University has right to use for non-commercial purposes	Sponsor
5	Contract research: no publication by university without Sponsor's permission	Sponsor

Which of these five agreements is used depends on the negotiating position of the parties and how much of the full economic cost (FEC) the sponsoring industrial partner is prepared to pay. In a letter to all UK Higher Education establishments dated 6 January 2005, Lord Sainsbury, Minister for Science and Innovation, and Dr. Kim Howells MP, Minister of State for Lifelong Learning, Further and Higher Education, introduced a summary statement of government policy on Higher Education research and sustainability.[17] This communication set the date for universities to apply full economic costing to research contracts. This means that universities, as in the business world, have to apply real costs to their research activities.

A good guide as to what may or may not be included in FEC can be found in the Dual Support Reform: Full Economic Costing, Guidance Notes for Peer Reviewers.[18] This demonstrated a clear intention by the UK government of the time that HEIs should take a stronger line in negotiating contracts with industry to ensure that charities and government were not unjustly subsidising for-profit companies. While the Lambert agreements have helped to standardise terms, which is useful to often under-resourced HEI research offices, the reality is that many HEIs will undervalue their research services or agree to less favourable terms to alleviate financial pressures or to build relationships with industry partners. Of course, as in any business, this flexibility is important, as long as it does not jeopardise the finances of the HEI.

Material transfer agreements

Material transfer agreements (MTAs) are far more insidious. The intention is that these agreements are used where regular, non-commercial, not-for-profit transfers of material take place, e.g. to a researcher in an HEI. Potentially there are three main parts to an MTA that may be considered areas of contention:

1. Definitions of the materials and the scope of their use.

2. Indemnifying the sender from liability to the receiver for the use of the materials when in the receiver's control and warrants relating to infringement and ownership.

3. Protecting the sender's interests in relation to existing or future IP arising from the use of the materials.

There will be other provisions for confidentiality, non-assignment, governing law, publication conditions, etc., but these are usually not as problematic.[19] The scope of the MTA is important to the operation of the agreement as it sets the boundaries of what the recipient researcher gets and what they can do with the materials (and results). The importance of adhering to the scope of use can be highlighted by the unfortunate Buffalo MTA case in the United States, in which two researchers were indicted for misuse of bacterial samples.[20] Unfortunately, the validity of the MTA was not actually tested as the case was precipitated by bioterrorism laws but it is still an interesting case that may serve to warn of the dangers of wandering beyond limits imposed by contract or law.

An MTA is not usually worth anything, the consideration for providing the materials is that the recipient abides by the terms and conditions of the MTA and pays the cost of shipping. However, the MTA has the potential to become valuable if any IP arises from the work done using the materials. The fact is that MTAs are the annoying red tape that academics think are right up to the point that someone takes legal action over an aspect of the agreement. As one would expect, the strictest IP clauses tend to come from industry, where the providing company will often claim all results and arising IP from work done. From their point of view the company may be protecting their rights over proprietary material, which is a perfectly understandable position but one that is probably an anti-competitive reach-through to independent research.[21]

The terms agreed in research contracts and MTAs without the input of a contract manager or, as sometimes happens, at the insistence of an impatient academic, can lead to serious conflicts that may arise with grant conditions. A major source of external funding for academics in the UK comes from charitable organisations and research councils; for example, UCL received £188 million in grant funding for the financial year 2009/2010 from charitable funders.[22] These funding bodies will impose obligations on the scientist and their institution alongside the award and this may include conditions relating to arising IP.

For instance, the Wellcome Trust's grant conditions[23] are very clear about their position on IP and a closer look at the Trust's policies show that there are instructions on how the IP should be exploited, licence terms that are required and the sharing of revenue back to the trust. This stance is not uncommon and is an example of how seriously charities take restrictions on their IP and how they recognise the importance of commercialising the results for the benefit of society. Basically, the interpretation is that any IP that comes out of grant-funded work needs to be *unencumbered*, free to commercialise by the university. In any case, where there is a transfer of IP or materials to a third party, contracts staff must, at the very least, ensure that the HEI and researcher(s) are able to continue to use them for ongoing research, even with other entities.

Conflicts of interest

One of the underlying currents technology transfer and contracts staff must be aware of throughout the negotiation of agreements is conflict of interest. Academic staff in most HEIs have the right to engage in external consultancy or other activities that might lead to them developing an interest in a company or IP that is potentially divergent to the ongoing interests of the HEI. In these cases it is important that the conflicts of interest policies are properly applied to ensure that the HEI's interests do not suffer. There are countless examples in every HEI of researchers entering (or inducing the HEI to enter) into contracts on the basis of a private interest, often short term in nature, to the long-term detriment of the HEI. Where the HEI (and in some cases the researchers themselves) can suffer the most is where the terms or existence of such an arrangement precludes or complicates the ability to conduct research in the field or to prevent the researcher applying for grants.

Patent reform

Lastly, I would like to explore a slightly radical idea to help alleviate another common problem encountered by HEI technology transfer offices: invention disclosures that arrive after the idea has been published. Ideally, at the back of every researcher's mind should be the question 'Is publication the only way my work can benefit society?' (preferably they should ask themselves this before they publish the idea). Most technology transfer offices survive on invention disclosures from less than 15% of academic staff, so imagine what could be done with more interaction; we are working hard to raise awareness and encourage involvement across the sector.[24]

At the moment, apart from educating researchers, there is not a lot that can be done to avoid pre-disclosures but perhaps in time an internationally-recognised academic grace period could be put in place to allow HEIs to file patents on IP that has been published. Until recently the US had a *first to invent* system whereby inventors were allowed a 12-month grace period within which to file a patent after disclosure of the invention to the public. Such a grace period would not necessarily be out of kilter with international patent laws as there are already limited grace periods in Canada, Japan and others, including in the European Patent Convention for inventions disclosed at specific trade shows (Article 55 (b)). Any grace period should be restricted to disclosures made by academic researchers in the course of their employment with an academic institution to ensure that there can be certainty for patent offices and users.

The potential costs of implementing and operating such a system may make this entirely unfeasible: there would be considerable diplomatic effort involved in changing the various treaties that govern national patent law and defining the eligibility, for example identifying an academic invention may be tricky in different territories. Some may see this as a retrograde step in the evolution of international patent law, particularly at a time when the United States Patent and Trademark Office is implementing a new first to file patent system but, along with better management of obligations, awareness of IP and strong technology transfer, I believe it would help make academic innovation an even more valuable contributor to the quality of life of millions.[25]

Recommended reading

Anderson, Mark (ed.), *Technology Transfer: Law and Practice* (Bloomsbury Professional, 2010)

Carlton, Dennis W. and Perloff, Jeffrey M., *Modern Industrial Organization* (Pearson, 2003)

PraxisUnico Practical Guides to Commercialisation:

www.praxisunico.org.uk/resources/practical-guides.asp

Endnotes

[1] HEFCE Good Research Practice FAQs, dated November 2011: **www.hefce.ac.uk/finance/charities/goodprac/faq.htm**

[2] RAE 2008 webpage: **www.rae.ac.uk**

[3] REF 2014 webpage: **www.hefce.ac.uk/research/ref**

[4] REF Research Impact Pilot Exercise Lessons-Learned Project: Feedback on Pilot Submissions, Technopolis Group Final Report for HEFCE published November 2010.

[5] See Campaign for Cambridge Freedoms: **www.cl.cam.ac.uk/~rja14/Papers/ccf-campaign.html**

[6] Report prepared by Professor Paul Wellings for the Secretary of State for Innovation, Universities and Skills (30 September 2008); 'Who owns science?', The Manchester Manifesto (2009).

[7] See Higher Education Innovation Fund Website: **www.hefce.ac.uk/econsoc/buscom/heif**

[8] J.C. Ginarte and W.C. Park demonstrated a correlation between a country's income and the strength of its IP laws in 'Determinants of Patent Rights: A Cross-National study', *Research Policy* 26 (1997).

[9] J. Hausman and G. Leonard, 'The Competitive Effects of a New Product Introduction: A Case Study' (2003) *Journal of Industrial Economics* 237-63 as quoted by O' Donoghue and Padilla and verified by the author.

[10] Building a Stronger Civil Society, Cabinet Office Paper 2010.

[11] IBIL Debate: Do Patents Incentivise or Inhibit Innovation, Senate House, London, 6 April 2011.

[12] Although how this might be a sustainable model is still not clear. For more information see the PraxisUnico press release dated 29 June 2011.

[13] An interesting examination of the principles and limits of academic freedom can be found in Eric Barendt's book, *Academic Freedom and the Law (A Comparative Study)*, Hart Publishing 2010.

[14] See **www.wellcome.ac.uk/Funding/Technology-transfer/Awards/Translation-Awards** for further information on these funds.

[15] Published December 2003.

[16] See **www.ipo.gov.uk/whyuse/research/lambert/lambert-mrc.htm**

[17] See copy here: **www.bis.gov.uk/policies/science/science-funding/full-economic-costing**

[18] See: **www.pparc.ac.uk/jes/dsr_peerreviewguidancev2.0.pdf**

[19] A useful guide to material transfer agreements and technology transfer practice in general is Mark Anderson's *Technology Transfer: Law and Practice* (Bloomsbury Professional, 2010).

[20] See: **www.the-scientist.com/news/20040809/03**

[21] It seems that one way companies may try to get around FEC is to put in place an onerous MTA with all the terms and obligations one would expect in a research contract but without funding. The company gets research on the cheap; the HEI gets all the responsibility.

[22] Reports and Financial Statements for the year ended 31 July 2010, UCL, compared with £12 million from industry for the same period.

[23] Wellcome Trust Cond10/11:
www.wellcome.ac.uk/stellent/groups/corporatesite/@sf_central_grants_admin/documents /web_document/wtx026668.pdf

[24] Analysis of UCLB' s activities in 09/10 and anecdotal evidence from other offices.

[25] The America Invents Act 2011.

10. University Patenting and the Advancement of Knowledge

By Catherine Rhodes

An introduction to the Manchester Manifesto

Who Owns Science? The Manchester Manifesto was launched in November 2009 by the Institute for Science, Ethics and Innovation at the University of Manchester.[1] It takes the form of a consensus statement of 50 academics from diverse fields including science, law, economics, bioethics and sociology, and includes two Nobel Laureates (Joseph Stiglitz and John Sulston). The Manifesto centres on a critique of the current dominant system of managing innovation on access to scientific information and the products of innovation because of the effects this system has:

> 'The current method of managing innovation (and perhaps particularly IP in its present form), whilst deeply embedded in current practice and hence of practical importance, also has significant drawbacks in terms of its effect on science and economic efficiency, and raises ethical issues because of its (often adverse) effects on people and populations.'[2]

The Manifesto is framed as a call for further investigation, action and policy change, rather than setting out solutions itself. While management of innovation is considered quite broadly, with several areas highlighted as problematic, its criticisms of the current patent system have been particularly

❝ University patenting should continue to have only a marginal role in university-industry relations in order to minimise damage to academic freedom and to safeguard the distinctive role of universities in knowledge systems. ❞

drawn out by readers (those both broadly critical and broadly supportive of the views expressed).

This chapter, written by one of the drafters of the Manifesto, draws on the critiques presented in that document but is designed to be more specific on the effects of patenting on academic research and the implications that increased university patenting has for the role of universities within innovation systems and for traditional academic freedoms and responsibilities.[3] It concludes that university patenting should continue to have only a marginal role in university-industry relations in order to minimise damage to academic freedom and to safeguard the distinctive role of universities in knowledge systems.

Currently, increased patenting of academic research is being promoted by governments, funding bodies and university management. This chapter focuses largely on the UK situation but also draws on studies from the United States and Europe.

Expectations and realities

Two major forms of benefit are predicted to result from the promotion of university patenting: financial benefits for universities; and technology transfer benefits for industry and wider society. The evidence for both is weak and most of the literature examining university-industry linkages and their impacts points to there being a general paucity of evidence forming the basis for policy in this area.[4]

Patenting activity is only likely to provide a significant stream of income for a minority of universities and will do so over the longer term rather than generating immediate financial benefit. For the majority of universities, revenue from patenting will barely cover expenditure. Data from the US, in which an expansion of university patenting began to be promoted several years earlier than in the UK, bears this out.

Some major American universities have gained substantial revenue from a few of their patents, but the majority have struggled to break even. Commentators have noted that the majority of US universities would get better returns on investment by placing money in government bonds or the state lottery.[5]

Lack of financial reward is not in itself sufficient reason to reject the value of patenting academic research and indeed does not appear to have been the main motivation behind policies promoting it. Instead this appears to have been facilitation of knowledge and technology transfer (KTT) to industry with resultant benefits to society.

KTT from universities to industry (and other groups outside academia) takes many forms, both formal and informal. These include publication of research in journals, delivery of papers at conferences, discussion of research through professional networks, release of data, exchange of personnel, collaborative projects and the provision of a graduate workforce.

The Higher Education Funding Council for England (HEFCE) conducts an annual survey of KTT activities from universities to the business community. It covers those activities to which monetary value can easily be assigned – patenting forms a very small percentage of this activity. The 2009-10 figures are summarised in Table 10.1.

Table 10.1 – summary of the figures from the HEFCE study of KTT activities for 2009-10

Activity	Income to Higher Education Institutions (£m)	Proportion of total (%)
IP income	84	2.6
Collaborative research income	749	24.2
Contract research income	983	31.8
Consultancy	362	11.7
Use of facilities/equipment	115	3.7
Continuing Professional Development	580	18.7
Regeneration	213	6.9
Total	3086	–

Source: HEFCE, September 2011. The figure for IP income is made up of licensing income of £58 million and sale of shares in spin-outs of £26 million. Expenditure on IP protection over this period was around £29 million.

A 2002 study also showed – from the perspective of industry – that publications, conferences, informal interactions and consultancy are all viewed as more important routes for KTT than patenting.[6]

The lack of importance of patenting with KTT may, again, not be sufficient reason to oppose increases in academic patenting. However, where patenting activity might conflict with other forms of KTT, for example by delaying presentation of research to colleagues, these costs should be carefully weighed. It also indicates that universities should avoid a narrow focus on patenting and pay greater attention to alternative forms of KTT that may be more effective and appropriate for particular cases.

From the university perspective there is no apparent need for increased patenting. It will rarely bring a significant return on expenditure and is a marginal form of transfer, which may push out other, more efficient forms. From an industry perspective it may still be beneficial. It may, for example, be important to decision making about whether to use the results of academic research and when to collaborate with universities, and it could give confidence about who owns and will receive reward from any resulting innovations. While patents might not be a significant source of income for universities, wider interactions with industry can be.

> **Where patenting activity might conflict with other forms of KTT, for example by delaying presentation of research to colleagues, these costs should be carefully weighed.**

There is not yet a substantial literature that examines university patenting from the perspective of industry. What there is indicates that, aside from the pharmaceutical and biomedical industries, relatively little importance is assigned to patenting and licensing as a route of KTT. For example, Cohen's 2002 study found that 'the most important channels of information flow between public research institutions and industrial R&D laboratories are the channels of open science, notably publications and public meetings and conferences'. Also, 'licences and patents are subordinate means of conveying the content of that research to industry' and that even in those few industries where university patenting is considered useful, 'informal channels and the channels of open science were still more important'.[7]

There are also studies which show that industry finds university approaches to IP negotiations problematic. Fabrizio reports that:

> 'Complaints include that transfer officers too aggressively protect the university's intellectual property, university policies are too cumbersome and rigid, and workers in the technology transfer offices may tend to be "inflexible and conservative" when negotiating licensing arrangements' and also that 'industry researchers report that delays due to negotiation of intellectual property rights can be significant, on the order of months.'[8]

Other studies found that aggressive university patenting contributed to a decline in industrial funding of US academic research[9] and a withdrawal of biotech firms from collaboration in Denmark following Bayh-Dole style reforms.[10] Examples of problems encountered include: negotiation being difficult and time-consuming; high demands for intellectual property rights and royalties; and disputes due to universities overvaluing intellectual property rights. Fabrizio's study also found:

> 'that an increase in university patenting is associated with a slow down in the pace of knowledge exploitation, measured as a lengthening of the average time between the creation of (patented) knowledge and the exploitation of this knowledge by a firm in new (patented) innovations.'[11]

The current strategies of governments, funders and universities thus seem flawed and there is substantial room for improvement.

Role of universities

Universities are designed to serve a particular role in society – that of advancing knowledge for public benefit and sharing that knowledge through education and other dissemination routes. In the UK and Europe, universities have received substantial public funding for at least the last 60 years because this role of knowledge advancement and dissemination is viewed as serving the public good.

Within knowledge and innovation systems there is good reason to have universities playing a distinct and complementary role to commercial enterprises. There is always likely to be some research, particularly basic research and research that produces public goods, that will be underserved by market incentives and public funding of university research is a good way to ensure this research is conducted.[12]

Glenna et al., for example, note that societies need provision of both private and public goods and this requires 'a division of labor between the private and public sectors' and 'different institutional structures have emerged to promote research oriented toward public and private outcomes'.[13] David argues that:

> 'neither system alone can perform as effectively over the long run as the two of them coupled together, since their special capabilities and limitations are complementary. Maintaining them in productive balance, therefore, is the central task towards which informed science and technology policies must be directed'.[14]

Preserving this distinctive role for universities requires that they be able to continue operating under different incentive schemes to industry. Increased use of patenting and other moves to commercial models for universities draws them into commercial incentive structures, encouraging them to respond to market forces.

Academic freedom

The role outlined above for universities, and the responsibilities they have for knowledge production and dissemination, exists alongside related academic freedoms. It has long been seen as important that academics be (as) free (as possible) from political, religious and other interference in their work. This logically extends to commercial influences.

Patenting of academic research can threaten academic freedom in two main ways:

1. It limits freedom to choose the direction of research; and

2. It limits freedom to disseminate research findings.

Freedom to choose the direction of research is valued because it is expected to enable selection based on expert understanding of the needs for and merits of particular avenues of research in line with the aim of advancing knowledge for societal benefit. An increased focus on patentability drives research in directions in which patents are more likely to be obtainable and have value in commercial terms. Sometimes this will coincide with lines of research that would have been chosen anyway, but there is widespread and justifiable concern that resources are being diverted from socially valuable areas of research that lack direct commercial value and that some lines of research may be abandoned altogether. These concerns have been particularly strongly expressed in the fields of agricultural and ecological research.[15]

Some industrial partners might be justified in favouring patentable research in their collaborations with universities, but it is worrying that some major public and charitable funders and universities themselves are pushing the same approach, because this means that funding sources for research not directed towards patentable results are becoming limited.

Freedom to share information on research activities and disseminate findings is fundamental to academic endeavour, which is inherently collective and cumulative in nature. It is, for example, a core part of scientific method that research be replicable so that others may test findings and judge their quality and significance. David explains that:

> 'production of knowledge which is "reliable" is fundamentally a social process' and there is 'incentive compatibility between the norm of disclosure and... a collegiate reputation-based reward system grounded upon validated claims to priority in discovery or innovation.'[16]

Most patent systems are set up on the basis that knowledge of the innovation must not be in the public domain at the time of application.[17] While disclosure is compulsory at the publication stage, knowledge-sharing is discouraged for a period of at least some months before filing. This blocks use of traditional dissemination routes prior to application, where a patent may be sought. Guidance from the UK Intellectual Property Office, for example, advises not to 'reveal your invention in any way – by word of mouth, demonstration, advertisement, article in a journal or any other way – before you apply for a patent'.[18] Delays to dissemination have been reported in several studies.[19]

There may also be restrictions on subsequent use of patented knowledge and tools in academic research. Research exemptions exist in some patent systems, however these will not apply where the intention is to commercialise the results of the further research. So, as university policy increasingly promotes patenting, the exemption loses its value – a point picked up on by the Intellectual Property Office in its advice to universities.[20]

It is clear that there are various problems presented for academic freedom by moves to increase university patenting activity. This again suggests that universities should modify their technology transfer policies, reducing the emphasis on patenting and seeking appropriate balance with safeguarding of academic freedoms and university autonomy.

Problems and recommendations

The above analysis points to there being little need to expand patenting of academic research and several reasons to avoid doing so. It also highlights a tension between the drive to increase university patenting and the fulfilment of academic responsibilities and protection of freedoms. This is not to say that all patenting of academic research is problematic. In some cases it could have value in alerting industry to particularly promising strands of research and in encouraging collaboration and investment.

A limited amount of university patenting targeted at areas with easily realisable commercial potential should not be too problematic. It would leave open the selection of productive lines of research by academics well-placed to judge their scientific and social merit. It would limit restrictions on exchange of data and knowledge within the academic community and from academia to industry, and so not clash significantly with other transfer routes. This is in line with Cohen et al.'s advice that:

> 'even when university-industry cooperative ventures or technology licensing… support technology transfer in an immediate way, encouragement of such bridging mechanisms should not come at the expense – as they occasionally do – of the other more important channels of open science.'[21]

❝ A limited amount of university patenting targeted at areas with easily realisable commercial potential should not be too problematic. ❞

There is a current imbalance in policy and practice which over-emphasises the importance of patenting and undervalues other transfer routes, academic freedom, and the distinctive role of universities in knowledge systems. This situation is not an inevitable outcome of current intellectual property law, but results from a combination of pressures from government, funders, technology transfer offices and university management, which are creating ever-stronger obligations for academics to patent (or at least maintain the option of patenting) their research.

At the governmental level, in the UK, these pressures have emerged alongside broader trends to reframe universities as commercial enterprises, which are problematic and inappropriate given the distinctive *public-good* role and responsibilities of universities. (The UK is not exceptional in this regard; similar policy shifts have occurred in many other European countries and in the US.)

There are some indications that government attitudes to academic patenting could be shifting, with, for example, David Willetts – Minister of State for Universities and Science – stating in a July 2010 speech 'Science, Innovation and the Economy' that:

> 'The challenge we face is to make best use of our science base. Especially in a time of austerity, we inevitably think of the way it can contribute to economic growth. I strongly believe that contribution may come best if we encourage openness and innovation, not if we try to micromanage our universities, direct researchers, or count patents.'

However, this is somewhat in tension with other government statements, for example Vince Cable – Secretary of State for Business Innovation and Skills – said in a September 2010 speech: 'This leads us on to the wider question of intellectual property and how we deal with it. Universities make only 5% of their externally earned income from patents and licensing… more needs to be done.'

Among the seven centrally resourced funding councils in the UK,[22] the Biotechnology and Biological Sciences Research Council (BBSRC) takes a particularly strong line in promoting patenting of research, encouraging its grantees to pursue patentable research outcomes and advising restrictions on information sharing to maintain patentability:

> 'BBSRC positively encourages the exploitation of the results of all research it sponsors at universities, colleges and research institutions, in order to enhance the competitiveness of UK industry and create wealth for the UK economy. Particular emphasis is, therefore, placed on the process of identifying and protecting intellectual property.' Also, they say 'Avoid any form of disclosure which could compromise the patentability of the invention.'[23]

There is some acknowledgement that such strategies can be problematic in regard to delaying dissemination of research findings, but no information is provided on alternative methods of protecting intellectual property and transferring knowledge and technology. It would be more appropriate – given their influence on what research is pursued from public funding – for the BBSRC to support recipients in having open choice of methods and modes of KTT and to provide adequate information on alternatives within and outside intellectual property rights protection. (BBSRC is currently revising its intellectual property guidance for researchers in line with its January 2012 Policy for Knowledge Exchange and Commercialisation.)[24]

> ❝ **University management and technology transfer offices (TTOs) are also placing unnecessary pressure on academics to conduct research that can be commercialised and to patent it. ❞**

Industrial partners that are funding or collaborating in university research may legitimately expect commercial returns on their input and investment, and for findings to be protected to ensure that such returns can be attained. Funding councils (and other not-for-profit funders) have neither reason nor need to expect financial returns on their funded research and they do not need it to be targeting commercial objectives. Grants from public funders ought to provide a separate incentive scheme to that which operates for industry, otherwise all research will ultimately become market driven, and significant social benefits will be lost. These funders have good reason therefore not to promote higher levels of university patenting and ought to adopt approaches that preserve the public good value of knowledge.

University management and technology transfer offices (TTOs) are also placing unnecessary pressure on academics to conduct research that can be commercialised and to patent it. TTOs do not generally have broad remits covering promotion of all types of KTT and appear to have limited capacity to assess and advise on which of the range of KTT options are most appropriate on a case-by-case basis. The role of TTOs should be interpreted as serving the broad needs and interests of universities (based on the roles, responsibilities and freedoms outlined earlier). This fits with the UK Intellectual Property Office's recent advice on university intellectual property strategy:

> 'In order to create the best environment for IP to be produced and transferred to practical use, a university must have a suite of IP policies and practices which reflect the university's mission. The policies have to sit in a complementary way with the core objective of knowledge creation, scholarship and learning.'[25]

TTOs and university management should listen and respond to the needs of academics in order to ensure that they do not unnecessarily complicate or delay future academic use of research results.

Universities and TTOs also need more realistic expectations of patenting in regard to the likelihood of gaining substantial revenues and to its importance in comparison with other forms of KTT. They should recognise that different universities will benefit from different approaches to IP protection – a point repeatedly emphasised in the Intellectual Property Office's 'Intellectual Asset Management for Universities'.

Universities vary greatly in their size and the type, scope and scale of research that their staff conduct. It is probably only a minority for which having a dedicated TTO is justified. Central higher education funding policy should also recognise these differences so that resourcing does not get skewed by rewarding only those universities that can attract significant KTT income. Similarly, greater understanding is needed about which types of research it is appropriate to seek patents on, at which stages and under what conditions. This should assist in making negotiations with industry easier.

Such altered strategies need not exclude patenting as a route to KTT, but they should not make it a priority goal of academic endeavour and in cases of conflict with other goals, the balance ought to be in favour of preserving the distinctive role of universities and fulfilment of academic freedoms and responsibilities.

Adjustments and alternatives

A range of initiatives have been developed in recent years to provide for adaptations or alternatives to standard intellectual property protection and which are generally better suited to the public interest missions of universities and traditions of open science. These include:

AUTM Global Health Initiative and Toolkit

The Association of University Technology Managers (AUTM) launched its Global Health Initiative and Toolkit in November 2009 to assist in the application of its Global Access Principles. The Initiative 'promotes licensing practices that support access to essential medicines by developing countries'[26] and aims to support universities 'in fostering public health' including through facilitation of 'the commercialization of health-related inventions of academic researchers by developing and disseminating these technologies for the public good' in a way which ensures 'that advances in health reach those who need them most'.[27] The toolkit includes example licensing clauses that have been used by universities.

UAEM Global Access Licensing Framework

Universities Allied for Essential Medicine (UAEM) is an international student organisation founded in Yale in 2001 with the aim of convincing universities to licence their medical innovations in ways that promote broad global access. UAEM's Global Access Licensing Framework takes a similar approach to the AUTM initiative, laying out principles for university licensing policy, rather than specifying particular licensing terms, with the goal of ensuring affordable access to medicines and medical technologies for low and middle-income countries.

Easy Access IP

Three UK universities (Bristol, Glasgow and Kings College London) with support from the Intellectual Property Office, launched an 'Easy Access Innovation Partnership' in early 2011. This gives companies free access to a selection of the universities' intellectual property with 'simple, one-page agreements: no lengthy or costly negotiation'. This initiative has met some criticism as providing nothing new and bringing little benefit.[28]

BioBricks

The BioBricks Foundation works in the area of synthetic biology promoting production of standardised biological parts to form the basis of the field. Because of the foundational nature of these parts, the Foundation believes that maintenance of free access to them is essential to the field's development. It has developed the BioBrick Public Agreement as a legal tool for institutional use to ensure that standardised biological parts remain in the public domain (**biobricks.org/bpa**).

Structural Genomics Consortium

The Structural Genomics Consortium (SGC) based in Oxford, Toronto and Stockholm, is 'a not-for-profit organisation that aims to determine the three-dimensional structures of proteins of medical relevance, and place them in the public domain without restriction'. It is a public-private partnership with funding from government, the Wellcome Trust, and industry partners. It has a completely open-access policy in relation to its work – no IP rights can be claimed. In this way, much duplication of effort within the pre-competitive stage of drug discovery is avoided and the probability of failure later in the development process is reduced (**www.sgc.ox.ac.uk**).[29]

Cambia/BiOS/Patentlens

Cambia is a non-profit organisation 'that invents and shares enabling technologies and new practices for life sciences and intellectual property to further social equity'. It has two major initiatives. BiOS (Biological Innovation for Open Society) involves a royalty-free licensing system and a 'protected commons' – a collaborative space for work on core technologies where confidentiality is maintained so that applications for patents on improvements are not blocked. Whether patented or not, all improvements are shared with the other licensees in the commons. Cambia also runs PatentLens, an informatics tool that can assist users in establishing freedom to operate (**www.patentlens.net**). It is a full-text searchable database of over 8 million patents and applications, accompanied by some landscaping studies, guides and tutorials.

Conclusions

The signs, for example from HEFCE's annual reports, are that the UK academic and business communities are quite effective and increasingly successful at transferring knowledge and technology through a variety of routes – even in times of general economic hardship. A recent study by academics at Imperial College estimated that UK academic research brought gains to the UK economy of £45 billion on a £3.5 billion spend over a year.[30]

Patenting of academic research need not be detrimental to academia. Currently, however, there is significant conflict between a drive to increase patenting and protection of academic freedoms, which needs to be addressed if universities are to continue to serve their particular role and fulfil their responsibilities.

It need not be particularly difficult to improve on current approaches to university IP. Changes are needed from government policy downwards – universities are unlikely to take significant steps if they fear it will further reduce income streams. These changes should be based on evidence about

❝ University TTOs should have their remits expanded to support all forms of KTT, knowing which are appropriate in particular cases and facilitating academic choice. ❞

the importance of patenting within a wide range of KTT activities and give full consideration to the roles that universities ought to play in knowledge and innovation systems – ensuring that research results, data and knowledge are as widely accessible and reusable as possible, and conducting research in areas in which the private sector lacks incentives.

There is a need for more realistic appreciation of the value and importance of patenting within the range of KTT activities available to academia and of the damage which an uninformed and inappropriately exclusive emphasis on producing patentable research can do to the advancement of knowledge within academia – knowledge that should, as much as possible, have its public good nature preserved. This implies less overall patenting activity by universities and more selectivity within this.

University TTOs should have their remits expanded to support all forms of KTT, knowing which are appropriate in particular cases and facilitating academic choice. There is scope for TTOs to learn from each other and develop best practice. New offices can learn from those with successful track records. For smaller universities or those that are less active in research, where limited income is expected, combined offices may be appropriate. Better understanding of flexibilities within and alternative models of protecting IP is needed, along with appreciation that in many cases public domain research will have greater overall benefit to academia, society and industry. Funders should adopt a similar approach, enabling recipients to choose from a range of options for protecting their IP, including open-access and public domain options, and being equally supportive of other forms of KTT, rather than encouraging a narrow focus on patenting. As D'Este & Patel state:

> 'if policies oriented to encouraging knowledge transfer activities are to succeed, support for a variety of interaction channels would seem to be more profitable as a route to building a solid integration between science and technology, rather than focussing on a narrowly defined set of commercialisation activities.'[32]

There also needs to be a shift back to more core public funding of universities, with recognition of their key social role and the public good nature of the knowledge and education they provide. This will reduce the pressures that are driving academic research to meet commercial goals and will facilitate more selective and appropriate IP strategies. This is, given the current economic climate, unlikely to occur in the short-term and may require difficult choices, such as a reduction in the number of universities. It is, however, vital in order to preserve the complementary nature of academia and industry within our knowledge-based economy, and it is a worthwhile investment as university research grounds innovation and contributes to economic growth – points which are also made by the OECD:

> 'the current economic environment raises a risk that governments will make policy and budgeting decisions that are not the best for the medium term and may harm innovation and longer-term prosperity. It is crucial to continue to invest in future long-term sources of growth such as education, infrastructure and research.'[33]

References

AUTM, Press Release – 'Association of University Technology Managers Announce New Global Health Initiative, Endorse Global Access Principles' (9 November 2009-1). Accessed 19 September 2011 through **www.autm.net/home**

AUTM, 'Statement of Principles and Strategies for the Equitable Dissemination of Medical Technologies', **www.autm.net/Content/NavigationMenu/TechTransfer/GlobalHealth/stat ementofprincliples.pdf** (9 November 2009-2). Accessed 19 September 2011.

BBSRC, 'Intellectual Property Policy', **www.bbsrc.ac.uk/web/FILES/Policies/intellectual_property_policy.pdf** (February 2005). Accessed 6 March 2012.

BBSRC, 'Policy for Knowledge Exchange and Commercialisation', **www.bbsrc.ac.uk/web/FILES/Policies/knowledge-exchange-commerciali sation-policy.pdf** (January 2012). Accessed 6 March 2012.

Bhattacharjee, Y., 'U.S. Research Funding: Industry Shrinks Academic Support', *Science* 312 (2006), p. 671.

BiOS, 'FAQs – What is Cambia?', **www.bios.net/daisy/bios/2462.html**. Accessed 17 August 2011.

BiOS. 'FAQs – BiOS Agreements', **www.bios.net/daisy/bios/faqs/faq-agreements.html**. Accessed 17 August 2011.

Bulut, H. and Moschini, G. 'U.S. universities' net returns from patenting and licensing: a quantile regression analysis', *Working Paper 06 –WP 432*, **www.card.iastate.edu/publications/DBS/PDFFiles/06wp432.pdf** (September 2006). Accessed 22 June 2010.

Cable, V., 'The role of science, research and innovation in creating growth'. Speech delivered at Queen Mary University of London, **www.bis.gov.uk/news/speeches/vince-cable-science-research-and-innova tion-speech** (8 September 2010). Accessed 16 August 2011.

Cohen, W.M., Nelson, R.R. and Walsh, J.P., 'Links and Impacts: The Influence of Public Research on Industrial R&D', *Management Science* 48:1 (2002), pp. 1-23.

Crespi, C., D'Este, P., Fontana, R. and Geuna, A. 2011. 'The impact of academic patenting on university research and its transfer', Research Policy, 40: 55-68.

David, 'The Economic Logic of "Open Science" and the Balance between Private Property Rights and the Public Domain in Scientific Data and Information: A Primer', in National Research Council, 'The Role of Scientific and Technical Data and Information in the Public Domain: Proceedings of a Symposium' (Washington D.C.: National Academies Press, 2003), pp. 19-34.

D'Este, P. and Patel, P., 'University-industry linkages in the UK: What are the factors underlying the variety of interactions with industry?', *Research Policy* 36 (2007), pp. 1295-1313.

Fabrizio, K.R., 'University patenting and the pace of industrial innovation', *Industrial and Corporate Change* (2007), pp.1-30. Downloaded from **icc.oxfordjournals.org**, 22 June 2010.

Franzoni, C. and Scellato, G., 'The grace period in international patent law and its effect on the timing of disclosure', *Research Policy* 39 (2010), pp. 200-213.

Geuna, A. and Nesta, L.J.J., 'University patenting and its effects on academic research: the emerging European evidence', *Research Policy* 35 (2006), pp. 790-807.

Glenna, L.L., Lacy, W.B., Welsh, R. and Biscotti, D., 'University administrators, agricultural biotechnology, and academic capitalism: Defining the public good to promote university-industry relationships', *The Sociological Quarterly* 48 (2007), pp. 141-163.

Gibbons, L.J., 'University innovation and technology transfer – the Bayh-Dole Act after 30 years of incentives to commercialize', presented at the 2009 Conference of the International Association for the Advance of Teaching and Research in Intellectual Property, **www.atrip.tf.vu.lt/docs/Paper_Gibbons. pdf** (September 2009). Accessed 22 June 2010.

Haskel, J. and Wallis, G., 'Public Support for innovation, intangible investment and productivity growth in the UK market sector, Discussion Paper 2010/1', Imperial College London Business School: **spiral.imperial.ac.uk/bitstream/10044/1/5280/1/Haskel%202010-01.pdf** (February 2010). Accessed 19 September 2011.

HEFCE, 'Higher Education – Business and Community Interaction Survey 2009-10', **www.hefce.ac.uk/pubs/hefce/2011/11_25** (September 2011). Accessed 17 September 2011.

Hockaday, T. and Naylor L., News Item: ' "Easy Access IP" – universities have been doing it for years': **www.isis-innovation.com/news/articles/EasyAccessIP.html** (May 2011).

Imperial College Business School, 'Press Release – University research contributes £45 billion a year to the UK economy according to new impact study', **www3.imperial.ac.uk/newsandeventspggrp/imperialcollege/ newssummary/news_16-3-2010-13-6-57** (16 March 2010). Accessed 23 June 2011.

iSEI, 'Who Owns Science? The Manchester Manifesto', **www.isei.manchester.ac.uk/TheManchesterManifesto.pdf** (November 2009). Accessed 17 September 2011.

Kings College London, 'Easy Access IP: A New Way to Share our Intellectual Property', **www.kcl.ac.uk/innovation/business/easyaccessip/index.aspx**. Accessed 16 August 2011.

Larsen, M.T., 'The implications of academic enterprise for public science: An overview of the empirical evidence', *Research Policy* 40 (2011), pp. 6-19.

National Science Foundation, 'Chapter 5: Academic Research and Development', Science and Engineering Indicators: 2010, **www.nsf.gov/stat istics/seind10/c5/c5h.htm** (2010). Accessed 24 September 2011.

OECD, 'Ministerial Report on the OECD Innovation Strategy: Innovation to Strengthen Growth and Address Global and Social Challenges – Key Findings', **www.oecd.org/dataoecd/51/28/45326349.pdf** (May 2010). Accessed 19 September 2011.

Structural Genomics Consortium, 'The Structural Genomics Consortium', **www.thesgc.org,** (April 2010). Accessed 21 September 2011.

Tinnemann, P., Ozbay, J., Saint V.A. and Willich, S.N., 'Patenting of university and non-university public research organisations in Germany: Evidence from patent applications for medical research results', *PLoS ONE*, 5:11 (2010).

Toleubayev, K., Jansen, K. and Van Huis, A., 'Commodification of science and the production of public goods: Plant protection research in Kazakhstan', *Research Policy* 39 (2010), pp. 411-421.

UK Intellectual Property Office, 'Intellectual Asset Management for Universities', **www.ipo.gov.uk/ipasset-management.pdf** (19 May 2011). Accessed 17 September 2011.

UK Intellectual Property Office, 'Patents – Basic Facts', **www.ipo.gov.uk/p-basicfacts.pdf** (July 2011). Accessed 22 September 2011.

Universities Allied for Essential Medicine, Global Access Licensing Framework v2.0.

essentialmedicine.org/archive/global-access-licensing-framework-galf-v20 (25 August 2011). Accessed 17 September 2011.

Valentin, F. and Jensen, R.L., 'Effects on academia-industry collaboration of extending university property rights', *Journal of Technology Transfer* 32:3 (2007), pp. 251-276.

Willetts, D., 'Science, Innovation and the Economy', speech delivered at Royal Institution, London. **www.bis.gov.uk/news/speeches/david-willetts-science-innovation-and-the-economy** (9 July 2010). Accessed 16 August 2011.

Zhen, Lei, Juneja, Rakhi and Wright, Brian D. 'Patents versus patenting: implications of intellectual property protection for biological research', *Nature Biotechnology* 27:1 (January 2009).

Endnotes

[1] www.isei.manchester.ac.uk/TheManchesterManifesto.pdf

[2] www.isei.manchester.ac.uk/TheManchesterManifesto.pdf, p.2.

[3] This chapter is not intended to be representative of the views of the consensus group as a whole, but represents the author's own opinions.

[4] For example: Crespi et al, 2011; D'Este & Patel, 2007; Franzoni & Scellato, 2011; Geuna & Nesta, 2006; Glenna et al, 2007; Tinneman et al, 2010.

[5] Bulut & Moschini, September 2006; Gibbons, September 2009.

[6] W. M. Cohen, R. R. Nelson and J. P. Walsh, 'Links and Impacts: The Influence of Public Research on Industrial R&D', *Management Science* 48:1 (2002), p. 17.

[7] W. M. Cohen, R. R. Nelson and J. P. Walsh, 'Links and Impacts: The Influence of Public Research on Industrial R&D', Management Science 48:1 (2002), pp. 16-17.

[8] K. R. Fabrizio, 'University patenting and the pace of industrial innovation', Industrial and Corporate Change (2007), p.7.

[9] Y. Bhattacharjee, 'U.S. Research Funding: Industry Shrinks Academic Support', *Science* 312 (2006). More recent data from the US appears to indicate that this trend from the early 2000s has reversed – see National Science Foundation (2010) Chapter 5.

[10] F. Valentin and R. L. Jensen, 'Effects on academia-industry collaboration of extending university property rights', *Journal of Technology Transfer* 32:3 (2007).

[11] K. R. Fabrizio, 'University patenting and the pace of industrial innovation', Industrial and Corporate Change (2007), p. 21.

[12] Several authors make this point – for example: David, 2003; Glenna et al, 2007, p.142; Larsen, 2011, p.6; Tinneman et al, 2010, p.10; Toleubayev et al, 2010, p.412.

[13] L. L. Glenna, W. B. Lacy, R. Welsh, and D. Biscotti, 'University administrators, agricultural biotechnology, and academic capitalism: Defining the public good to promote university-industry relationships', *The Sociological Quarterly* 48 (2007), p. 142.

[14] P. David, 'The Economic Logic of "Open Science" and the Balance between Private Property Rights and the Public Domain in Scientific Data and Information: A Primer', in National Research Council, 'The Role of Scientific and Technical Data and Information in the Public Domain: Proceedings of a Symposium' (Washington D.C.: National Academies Press, 2003), p. 23.

[15] Glenna, 'University administrators'; and K. Toleubayev, K. Jansen and A. Van Huis, 'Commodification of science and the production of public goods: Plant protection research in Kazakhstan', *Research Policy*, 39 (2010).

[16] David, 'Open Science', p. 21.

[17] There are a few exceptions. The US for example has a general grace period, permitting disclosure within 12 months before filing (Franzoni & Scellato, 2007, p.200). There is an apparent link between use of the grace period and earlier disclosure of academic innovations (10.6 months before, compared to 16.1 months after filing) and to higher quality patents, probably due to refinement during the grace period (Franzoni & Scellato, 2007, p.201).

[18] UK Intellectual Property Office, 'Patents – Basic Facts' (July 2011), p.5.

[19] Including Crespi et al, 2011; Franzoni & Scellato, 2010; Geuna & Nesta, 2006; and Zhen et al, 2009.

[20] UK Intellectual Property Office, 'Intellectual Asset Management for Universities' (May 2011), p.28.

[21] Cohen, 'Links and Impacts', p. 22.

[22] The UK research councils are: the Arts and Humanities Research Council; Biotechnology and Biological Sciences Research Council; Economic and Social Research Council; Engineering and Physical Sciences Research Council; Medical Research Council; Natural Environment Research Council; and the Science and Technology Facilities Council.

[23] BBSRC, 'Intellectual Property Policy' (February 2005), pp. 5-7.

[24] BBSRC, 'Policy for Knowledge Exchange and Commercialisation' (January 2012).

[25] UK Intellectual Property Office, 'Intellectual Asset Management', p. 3.

[26] AUTM, 9 November 2009-1.

[27] AUTM, 9 November 2009-2.

[28] T. Hockaday and L. Naylor, News Item: ' "Easy Access IP" – universities have been doing it for years', May 2011.

[29] Structural Genomics Consortium, 'The Structural Genomics Consortium' (April 2010).

[30] Imperial College Business School. Press Release – 'University research contributes £45 billion a year to the UK economy according to new impact study' (16 March 2010); J. Haskel and G. Wallis, 'Public Support for innovation, intangible investment and productivity growth in the UK market sector', Discussion Paper 2010/1, Imperial College London Business School (February 2010).

[31] P. D'Este and P. Patel, 'University-industry linkages in the UK: What are the factors underlying the variety of interactions with industry?', *Research Policy* 36 (2007), p. 1310.

[32] OECD, 'Ministerial Report on the OECD Innovation Strategy: Innovation to Strengthen Growth and Address Global and Social Challenges – Key Findings', (May 2010), p. 2.

11. Some Final Thoughts

By Graham Richards

There is little doubt that the exploitation of university intellectual property is here to stay, indeed it is likely that the practice will become more widespread. Financial pressures on universities and the desire of governments to see a return on their investment that includes the creation of jobs, new industries and an improvement in the lives of their citizens make this development inevitable, as does the imperative for universities to demonstrate their impact.

Concomitantly, as we have seen in this book, issues arise – whether the commercialisation of intellectual property impacts upon the freedom of academics to research problems of their own choice or takes funding away from curiosity-driven research areas towards the more overtly commercial. Academic freedom is important and it is vital that commercialisation activity remains commensurate with the abiding principles of universities whilst creating a fair and convenient path to exploitation.

Universities need to put policies in place to ensure that abuses are avoided. It is important that the ownership of intellectual property is clear and is codified in the contracts of researchers. The best approach is for the university to hold the title, including the work performed by students as part of research for

“ **Academic freedom is important and it is vital that commercialisation activity remains commensurate with the abiding principles of universities whilst creating a fair and convenient path to exploitation.** ”

higher degrees. For this to be acceptable there has to be an equitable distribution of any income generated, perhaps with incentives to encourage protection prior to publication. University policies should include provision for researchers, departments, the central bodies and outside companies to resolve questions of conflict of interest or other grievances. This is preferably done by mediation and arbitration rather than recourse to the courts – to this end the maintenance of a precedents book is wise. It would also help if academics and their institutions kept better records.

Governments could help by encouraging the standardisation of ownership of intellectual property and encouraging universal patterns of financial return and compensation. This would be particularly helpful when different institutions collaborate, as well as making negotiation with industrial companies simpler. The provision of template agreements which universities could choose to adopt would be a significant step forward.

It is important not to overstate the financial return likely to accrue to universities. There may be rare huge winners, but in general the rewards are likely to be modest and have to be balanced against the not inconsiderable costs of protection and delaying presentation of research to colleagues. For this reason it may be wise for different institutions to collaborate as it may be difficult for a single technology transfer office to have expertise in every field of research. Sharing facilities between campuses should be considered, although having a patent attorney close to the research has a clear benefit. To assist collaboration some generic forms of terms of agreement would again be of help, including clear and universal principles of compensation.

The question of universities owning the copyright of works published by their employees is certain to be highly contentious, but in fairness has many parallels with the research of scientists when involving the subject for which a given academic is paid to teach and research. Copyright, along with income from consulting and other income generated by researchers, should also be considered. Perhaps, as with licensing of intellectual property, all initial income should go to the academic, but an increasing percentage should go to the university if this return becomes very large.

Students are attracted by and excited by the exploitation of intellectual property, so there are educational opportunities in teaching entrepreneurship. Similarly, academics should be educated about technology transfer, patents and commercialisation. In my experience, case studies are well received as an introduction.

It is still the case that more than 90% of discoveries never make the transition to the real world. One reason for this is that the application is not always obvious. To address this problem, a group of Oxford students have set up Marblar (**www.marblar.com**). The intention is to use crowd sourcing for ideas – the worldwide community is invited to suggest applications for technology and these can be voted upon to find the best or most novel possibility. Already this has led to discussions about new start-up companies.

We have come a long way from the era when academics thought that commercialisation was almost a grubby activity, but we need to ensure that the pendulum does not swing too far in the opposite direction. Academics should be hired on the basis of their research and teaching capabilities, without consideration as to whether their work might be commercially exploitable. All experience shows that the big successes have come from blue-sky research; predicting the future is very difficult. Academics should be encouraged to consider patenting and exploiting their research, but not forced to do so.

Above all academics should be encouraged to ask themselves in what way their research may be of most significant impact and most benefit to society. This may be by disseminating knowledge freely, but increasingly the answer may be by exploiting the intellectual property.

Index

E

F

G

H

I

J

K

L